CHILDREN IN NEED OF SUPPORT

JOANNE WESTWOOD

palgrave
macmillan

First published 2014 by
PALGRAVE MACMILLAN

Palgrave Macmillan in the UK is an imprint of Macmillan Publishers
Limited,registered in England, company number 785998, of Houndmills,
Basingstoke,Hampshire RG21 6XS.

Palgrave Macmillan in the US is a division of St Martin's Press LLC,
175 Fifth Avenue, New York, NY 10010.

Palgrave Macmillan is the global academic imprint of the above companies
and has companies and representatives throughout the world.

Palgrave® and Macmillan® are registered trademarks in the United
States, the United Kingdom, Europe and other countries

ISBN: 978–1–137–28658–1

This book is printed on paper suitable for recycling and made from fully
managed and sustained forest sources. Logging, pulping and manufacturing
processes are expected to conform to the environmental regulations of
the country of origin.

A catalogue record for this book is available from the British Library.

A catalog record for this book is available from the Library of Congress.

Typeset by Cambrian Typesetters, Camberley, Surrey

Printed in China

For my children Bruce, Louise and Jake

CONTENTS

TABLE OF CASES

TABLE OF STATUTES AND REGULATIONS

ACKNOWLEDGMENTS

I am very grateful to a group of BA social work students who read early draft chapters of this book and provided me with valuable feedback: Mark Barlow, Michelle Robinson, Olajumoke Omisore, Petra Celestine, Rebecca Evans, Tanya Whiles Todd Cooke, Wendy Smith and Helen Richards.

I would like to thank my former colleague Eileen Houghton for her encouragement and support, Peter Yates at the University of Edinburgh who is undertaking research about sibling incest, and Helen Kane who is an Enhanced Family Court Advisor with CAFCASS and a former YOT worker. Peter and Helen answered questions about the application of the law and provided me with useful resources for Chapter 7.

ABBREVIATIONS

ADHD	attention deficit and hyperactivity disorder
CAF	Common Assessment Framework
CAFCASS	Children and Family Court Advisory and Support Service
CPAG	Child Poverty Action Group
CSDPA	Chronically Sick and Disabled Persons Act 1970
DfE	Department for Education
DfES	Department for Education and Skills
DH	Department of Health
ECHR	European Convention on Human Rights
EHRC	Equality and Human Rights Commission
FGC	family group conferencing
IMCA	Independent Mental Capacity Advocate
LAC review	looked after child review
LASSA	Local Authority Social Services Act 1970
LEA	Local Education Authority
LFF	Lucy Faithfull Foundation
LSCB	Local Safeguarding Children Board
MAPPA	multi-agency public protection arrangements
NYAS	National Youth Advocacy Service
NGO	non-governmental organization
NSPCC	National Society for the Prevention of Cruelty to Children
OFSTED	Office for Standards in Education
PTC	primary care trust
PTSD	post-traumatic stress disorder
UASCs	Unaccompanied asylum seeking children
UKBA	UK Border Authority
UNCRC	United Nations Convention on the Rights of the Child
YJB	Youth Justice Board
YOI	Young Offenders Institution
YOT	Youth Offending Team

USING THIS BOOK

Aim of the series

Welcome to the Focus on Social Work Law Series.

This introductory section aims to elucidate the aims and philosophy of the series; introduce some key themes that run through the series; outline the key features within each volume; and offer a brief legal skills guide to complement use of the series.

The Social Work Law Focus Series provides a distinct range of specialist resources for students and practitioners. Each volume provides an accessible and practical discussion of the law applicable to a particular area of practice. The length of each volume ensures that whilst portable and focused there is nevertheless a depth of coverage of each topic beyond that typically contained in comprehensive textbooks addressing all aspects of social work law and practice.

Each volume includes the relevant principles, structures and processes of the law (with case law integrated into the text) and highlights clearly the application of the law to practice. A key objective for each text is to identify the policy context of each area of practice and the factors that have shaped the law into its current presentation. As law is constantly developing and evolving, where known, likely future reform of the law is identified. Each book takes a critical approach, noting inconsistencies, omissions and other challenges faced by those charged with its implementation.

The significance of the Human Rights Act 1998 to social work practice is a common theme in each text and implications of the Act for practice in the particular area are identified with inclusion of relevant case law.

The series focuses on the law in England and Wales. Some references may be made to comparable aspects of law in Scotland and Northern Ireland, particularly to highlight differences in approach. With devolution in Scotland and the expanding role of the Welsh Assembly Government it will be important for practitioners in those areas and working at the borders to be familiar with any such differences.

Features

At a glance content lists

Each chapter begins with a bullet point list summarizing the key points within the topic included in that chapter. From this list the reader can see 'at a glance' how the materials are organized and what to expect in that section. The introductory chapter provides an overview of the book, outlining coverage in each chapter that enables the reader to see how the topic develops throughout the text. The boundaries of the discussion are set including, where relevant, explicit recognition of areas that are excluded from the text.

Key case analysis

One of the key aims of the series is to emphasize an integrated understanding of law, comprising legislation and case law and practice. For this reason each chapter includes at least one key case analysis feature focusing on a particularly significant case. The facts of the case are outlined in brief followed by analysis of the implications of the decision for social work practice in a short commentary. Given the significance of the selected cases, readers are encouraged to follow up references and read the case in full together with any published commentaries.

On-the-spot questions

These questions are designed to consolidate learning and prompt reflection on the material considered. These questions may be used as a basis for discussion with colleagues or fellow students and may also prompt consideration or further investigation of how the law is applied within a particular setting or authority, for example, looking at information provided to service users on a council website. Questions may also follow key cases, discussion of research findings or practice scenarios, focusing on the issues raised and application of the relevant law to practice.

Practice focus

Each volume incorporates practice-focused case scenarios to demonstrate how the law is applied to social work practice. The scenarios may be fictional or based on an actual decision.

Further reading

Each chapter closes with suggestions for further reading to develop knowledge and critical understanding. Annotated to explain the reasons for inclusion, the reader may be directed to classic influential pieces, such as enquiry reports, up-to-date research and analysis of issues discussed in the chapter, and relevant policy documents. In addition students may wish to read in full the case law included throughout the text and to follow up references integrated into discussion of each topic.

Websites

As further important sources of information, websites are also included in the text with links from the companion website. Some may be a gateway to access significant documents including government publications, others may provide accessible information for service users or present a particular perspective on an area, such as the voices of experts by experience. Given the rapid development of law and practice across the range of topics covered in the series, reference to relevant websites can be a useful way to keep pace with actual and anticipated changes

Glossary

Each text includes a subject-specific glossary of key terms for quick reference and clarification. A flashcard version of the glossary is available on the companion website.

Visual aids

As appropriate, visual aids are included where information may be presented accessibly as a table, graph or flow chart. This approach is particularly helpful for the presentation of some complex areas of law and to demonstrate structured decision-making or options available.

Companion site

The series-wide companion site www.palgrave.com/socialworklaw provides additional learning resources, including flashcard glossaries, web links, a legal skills guide, and a blog to communicate important developments and updates. The site will also host a student feedback zone.

Key sources of law

In this section an outline of the key sources of law considered through-out the series is provided. The following 'Legal skills' section includes some guidance on the easiest ways to access and understand these sources.

Legislation

The term legislation is used interchangeably with Acts of Parliament and statutes to refer to primary sources of law.

All primary legislation is produced through the parliamentary process, beginning its passage as a Bill. Bills may have their origins as an expressed policy in a government manifesto, in the work of the Law Commission, or following and responding to a significant event such as a child death or the work of a government department such as the Home Office.

Each Bill is considered by both the House of Lords and House of Commons, debated and scrutinized through various committee stages before becoming an Act on receipt of royal assent.

Legislation has a title and year, for example, the Equality Act 2010. Legislation can vary in length from an Act with just one section to others with over a hundred. Lengthy Acts are usually divided into headed 'Parts' (like chapters) containing sections, subsections and paragraphs. For example, s. 31 of the Children Act 1989 is in Part IV entitled 'Care and Supervision' and outlines the criteria for care order applications. Beyond the main body of the Act the legislation may also include 'Schedules' following the main provisions. Schedules have the same force of law as the rest of the Act but are typically used to cover detail such as a list of legislation which has been amended or revoked by the current Act or detailed matters linked to a specific provision, for instance, Schedule 2 of the Children Act 1989 details specific services (e.g. day centres) which may be provided under the duty to safeguard and promote the welfare of children in need, contained in s. 17.

Remember also that statutes often contain sections dealing with inter-pretation or definitions and, although often situated towards the end of the Act, these can be a useful starting point.

Legislation also includes Statutory Instruments which may be in the form of rules, regulations and orders. The term delegated legislation collectively describes this body of law as it is made under delegated authority of Parliament, usually by a minister or government department. Statutory Instruments tend to provide additional detail to the outline scheme provided by the primary legislation, the Act of Parliament. Statutory Instruments are usually cited by year and a number, for example, Local Authority Social Services (Complaints Procedure) Order SI 2006/1681.

Various documents may be issued to further assist with the implementation of legislation including guidance and codes of practice.

Guidance

Guidance documents may be described as formal or practice guidance. Formal guidance may be identified as such where it is stated to have been issued under s. 7(1) of the Local Authority Social Services Act 1970, which provides that 'local authorities shall act under the general guidance of the Secretary of State'. An example of s. 7 guidance is *Working Together to Safeguard Children* (2013, London: Department of Health). The significance of s. 7 guidance was explained by Sedley J in *R v London Borough of Islington, ex parte Rixon* [1997] ELR 66: 'Parliament in enacting s. 7(1) did not intend local authorities to whom ministerial guidance was given to be free, having considered it, to take it or leave it … in my view parliament by s. 7(1) has required local authorities to follow the path charted by the Secretary of State's guidance, with liberty to deviate from it where the local authority judges on admissible grounds that there is good reason to do so, but without freedom to take a substantially different course.' (71)

Practice guidance does not carry s. 7 status but should nevertheless normally be followed as setting examples of what good practice might look like.

Codes of practice

Codes of practice have been issued to support the Mental Health Act 1983 and the Mental Capacity Act 2005. Again, it is a matter of good practice to follow the recommendations of the codes and these lengthy documents include detailed and illustrative scenarios to assist with interpretation and application of the legislation. There may also be a duty on specific people charged with responsibilities under the primary legislation to have regard to the code.

Guidance and codes of practice are available on relevant websites, for example, the Department of Health, as referenced in individual volumes.

Case law

Case law provides a further major source of law. In determining disputes in court the judiciary applies legislation. Where provisions within legislation are unclear or ambiguous the judiciary follows principles of statutory interpretation but at times judges are quite creative.

Some areas of law are exclusively contained in case law and described as common law. Most law of relevance to social work practice is of relatively recent origin and has its primary basis in legislation. Case law remains relevant as it links directly to such legislation and may clarify and explain provisions and terminology within the legislation. The significance of a particular decision will depend on the position of the court in a hierarchy whereby the Supreme Court is most senior and the Magistrates' Court is junior. Decisions of the higher courts bind the lower courts – they must be followed. This principle is known as the doctrine of precedent. Much legal debate takes place as to the precise element of a ruling which subsequently binds other decisions. This is especially the case where in the Court of Appeal or Supreme Court there are between three and five judges hearing a case, majority judgments are allowed and different judges may arrive at the same conclusion but for different reasons. Where a judge does not agree with the majority, the term dissenting judgment is applied.

It is important to understand how cases reach court. Many cases in social work law are based on challenges to the way a local authority has exercised its powers. This is an aspect of administrative law known as judicial review where the central issue for the court is not the substance of the decision taken by the authority but the way it was taken. Important considerations will be whether the authority has exceeded its powers, failed to follow established procedures or acted irrationally.

Before an individual can challenge an authority in judicial review it will usually be necessary to exhaust other remedies first, including local authority complaints procedures. If unsatisfied with the outcome of a complaint an individual has a further option which is to complain to the Local Government Ombudsman (LGO). The LGO investigates alleged cases of maladministration and may make recommendations to local authorities including the payment of financial compensation. Ombudsman decisions may be accessed on the LGO website and make interesting reading. In cases involving social services, a common concern across children's and adults' services is unreasonable delay in carrying out assessments and providing services. See www.lgo.org.uk.

Classification of law

The above discussion related to the sources and status of laws. It is also important to note that law can serve a variety of functions and may be grouped into recognized classifications. For law relating to social work practice key classifications distinguish between law which is criminal or civil and law which is public or private.

Whilst acknowledging the importance of these classifications, it must also be appreciated that individual concerns and circumstances may not always fall so neatly into the same categories, a given scenario may engage with criminal, civil, public and private law.

- Criminal law relates to alleged behaviour which is defined by statute or common law as an offence prosecuted by the state, carrying a penalty which may include imprisonment. The offence must be proved 'beyond reasonable doubt'.
- Civil law is the term applied to all other areas of law and often focuses on disputes between individuals. A lower standard of proof, 'balance of probabilities', applies in civil cases.
- Public law is that in which society has some interest and involves a public authority, such as care proceedings.
- Private law operates between individuals, such as marriage or contract.

Legal skills guide: accessing and understanding the law

Legislation

Legislation may be accessed as printed copies published by The Stationery Office and is also available online. Some books on a particular area of law will include a copy of the Act (sometimes annotated) and this is a useful way of learning about new laws. As time goes by, however, and amendments are made to legislation it can become increasingly difficult to keep track of the up-to-date version of an Act. Revised and up-to-date versions of legislation (as well as the version originally enacted) are available on the website www.legislation.gov.uk.

Legislation may also be accessed on the Parliament website. Here, it is possible to trace the progress of current and draft Bills and a link to Hansard provides transcripts of debates on Bills as they pass through both Houses of Parliament, www.parliament.uk.

Bills and new legislation are often accompanied by 'Explanatory notes' which can give some background to the development of the new law and offer useful explanations of each provision.

Case law

Important cases are reported in law reports available in traditional bound volumes (according to court, specialist area or general weekly reports) or online. Case referencing is known as citation and follows particular conventions according to whether a hard copy law report or online version is sought.

Citation of cases in law reports begins with the names of the parties, followed by the year and volume number of the law report, followed by an abbreviation of the law report title, then the page number. For example: *Lawrence v Pembrokeshire CC* [2007] 2 FLR 705. The case is reported in volume 2 of the 2007 Family Law Report at page 705.

Online citation, sometimes referred to as neutral citation because it is not linked to a particular law report, also starts with the names of the parties, followed by the year in which the case was decided, followed by an abbreviation of the court in which the case was heard, followed by a number representing the place in the order of cases decided by that court. For example: *R (Macdonald) v Royal Borough of Kensington and Chelsea* [2011] UKSC 33. Neutral citation of this case shows that it was a 2011 decision of the Supreme Court.

University libraries tend to have subscriptions to particular legal databases, such as 'Westlaw', which can be accessed by those enrolled as students, often via direct links from the university library webpage. Westlaw and LexisNexis are especially useful as sources of case law, statutes and other legal materials. Libraries usually have their own guides to these sources, again often published on their websites. For most cases there is a short summary or analysis as well as the full transcript.

As not everyone using the series will be enrolled at a university, the following website can be accessed without any subscription: BAILLI (British and Irish Legal Information Institute) www.bailii.org. This site includes judgments from the full range of UK court services including the Supreme Court, Court of Appeal and High Court but also features a wide range of tribunal decisions. Judgments for Scotland, Northern Ireland and the Republic of Ireland are also available as are judgments of the European Court of Human Rights.

Whether accessed via a law report or online, the presentation of cases follows a template. The report begins with the names of the parties, the court which heard the cases, names(s) of the judges(s) and dates of the hearing. This is followed by a summary of key legal issues involved in the case (often in italics) known as catchwords, then the headnote, which is a paragraph or so stating the key facts of the case and the nature of the claim or dispute or the criminal charge. 'HELD' indicates the ruling of the court. This is followed by a list of cases that were referred to in legal argument during the hearing, a summary of the journey of the case through appeal processes, names of the advocates and then the start of the full judgment(s) given by the judge(s). The judgment usually recounts the circumstances of the case, findings of fact and findings on the law and reasons for the decision.

If stuck on citations the Cardiff Index to Legal Abbreviations is a useful resource at www.legalabbrevs.cardiff.ac.uk.

There are numerous specific guides to legal research providing more detailed examination of legal materials but the best advice on developing legal skills is to start exploring the above and to read some case law – it's surprisingly addictive!

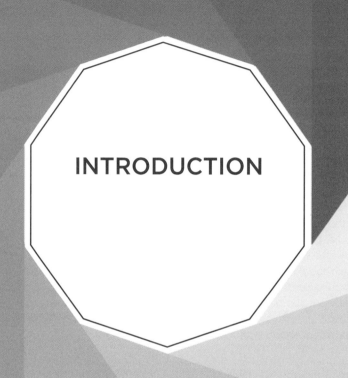

INTRODUCTION

This book discusses the legislation as it relates to **children in need** of support. It is designed to assist students and practitioners to understand how the legislation and policy governs social work practice with children in need. The College of Social Work in its *Curriculum Guide* (Braye and Preston-Shoot, 2012) to social work law stipulates that a focus on law should be maintained throughout social work training and not simply located in one module and, as such, this book is designed to be used across social work training and in the immediate post-qualifying professional development phase.

There is much uncertainty in social work practice with children, young people and their families. As in other areas of social work, interventions and support regarding children in need is governed by practice guidance and legislation. When social work comes under scrutiny and is accused of failing to protect or intervene, as illustrated in high-profile cases such as the deaths of Peter Connolly in 2007 or Daniel Pelka in 2012, the media, politicians and other public commentators raise questions about how abuse or harm was missed, and how it could have been prevented. Much social work in practice with children and their families begins with *assessing needs*. The categorization of children as being *in need* requires a different approach and emphasis than is found in the risk identification, assessment and management that characterizes child protection and child safeguarding work.

The Children Act 1989

Although the Children Act 1989 first introduced the concept of children in need, much post-war child care legislation in the UK recognized that early identification and support to children and their families could prevent children coming into the care of local authorities or their drifting into the juvenile justice system. The Child Care Act 1980 placed a duty on local authorities to provide assistance and guidance to families and to promote the welfare of children. When it was introduced one of the principle aims of the Children Act 1989 was to prioritize the welfare of children, wherever possible in the family, and, in terms of children in need, to place a duty on local authorities to promote the welfare of such children in their areas.

Part III of the Children Act 1989 outlines the duties, powers and responsibilities of local authorities to identify children in need and implement measures to promote their welfare.

s. 17

(1) It shall be the general duty of every local authority (in addition to the other duties imposed on them by this Part)—
  (a) to safeguard and promote the welfare of children within their area who are in need; and
  (b) so far as is consistent with that duty, to promote the upbringing of such children by their families.

Children Act 1989

Section 17(4) requires the local authority to:

s. 17(4)

  (a) ascertain the child's wishes and feelings regarding the provision of those services; and
  (b) give due consideration (having regard to his age and understanding) to such wishes and feelings of the child as they have been able to ascertain.

Children Act 1989

Section 17(10) defines who is a **child in need**:

s. 17(10)

For the purposes of this Part a child shall be taken to be in need if:

  (a) he is unlikely to achieve or maintain, or to have the opportunity of achieving or maintaining, a reasonable standard of health or development without the provision for him of services by a local authority under this Part;
  (b) his health or development is likely to be significantly impaired, or further impaired, without the provision for him of such services; or
  (c) he is disabled,

and 'family', in relation to such a child, includes any person who has parental responsibility for the child and any other person with whom he has been living.

Children Act 1989

The role of the state in terms of achieving a balance in interventions in family life had been an ongoing tension which erupted periodically during the 1980s. During this period there was as a growing lobby of activity from parents' groups and organizations who called for an emphasis on working in partnership with parents. The adversarial and authoritarian approach which was prevalent in the post-war period was rejected by this lobby (Hendrick, 1994). Whilst it had been recognized in previous legislation that there were children who required support from the state but not necessarily protection, the definition in the Children Act 1989 introduced and defined who children in need are and what parents and local authorities' duties, powers and responsibilities are towards these children. The Children Act 1989 can therefore be said to have institutionalized the concept of children in need.

Social workers in child protection and safeguarding services are described as overwhelmed by the enormity and complexity in their case loads (Turney et al., 2011). These aspects of children's social work are given high priority through policy and practice in, for example, the establishment of Local Safeguarding Children Boards (LSCBs) and other local procedures. Social work with children in need and their families is equally complex and challenging although it is less likely to gain political and public attention and is seen as a lesser priority. As can be seen from the various public inquiries, serious case reviews and volumes of research and evidence in the last 30 years, early intervention work with children and families can, in many instances, prevent the escalation of problems and provide a pathway to support for families who may need this intermittently.

The Children Act 1989 introduced a set of principles on which the law relating to the welfare of children, and the state's role in intervening in family life, should be based. This key piece of legislation, along with several other statutes, shapes a broad system of support for children and their families. However, the resources which are available to social workers to provide and enable families to access support are finite and the legislation and guidance also define who can access support and under what conditions.

Children and young people also have rights and entitlements. As well as being children they are also citizens and, as such, their roles as dependents and recipients of welfare are not straightforward (Montgomery and Kellett, 2009). This book includes discussion of the relevance of the articles contained within the **United Nations Convention on the Rights of the Child** (UNCRC) (UN Committee on the Rights of the Child, 2008) and examples of practice and support for children in need and their families which emphasize the role of community-based family support mechanisms.

Who are children in need?

The **Children in Need Annual Census** is an annual collection of data that covers all children who are referred to children's social care services, even if no further action is taken. The census includes children who are looked after, those supported in their families or independently and children who are the subject of a child protection plan. For the purpose of the census, a child in need is defined as one who has been assessed by children's social care to be in need of services. These services can include accommodation, respite, family support to help keep together families who are experiencing difficulties, the provision of support to those who are leaving or have left local authority care, adoption support, or disabled children's services (DfE, 2013a). At 31 March 2012, the number of children in need was 369,400 a decrease from the previous year (382,400). The rate per 10,000 children aged less than 18 years was 325.

These annual statistics are gathered to estimate and plan for children in need at a national level, although there are some issues about the way in which children in need are defined and counted at a local level. As outlined above the statistics collated for the census include all children referred and looked after and those who are subject to a safeguarding intervention – this is a broader group of children than the Children Act 1989 intended to be classified as in need and, in practice, social workers may consider children in need as those who are receiving support services but are not subject to other statutory interventions.

In relation to the definition of children with disabilities as being 'in need' the children with disabilities register which local authorities are required to maintain does not include children with diagnosed emotional and behavioural problems, or with dyspraxia/dyslexia. It is these groups of children who may have additional needs which universal services cannot meet and who require services and support from local authorities. In addition parents who have a child with a disability may opt not to register their child on the register and local authorities have been criticized for failing to maintain a register. As such the statistics can never be definitive but only an indicator and the process of assessment of need requires an understanding of how child care legislation defines and determines who is a child 'in need'.

There are arguments from child welfare campaigners which suggest that children in need are a wider group than those who meet the legal definition. The Child Poverty Action Group (CPAG), for example, argues that poverty is more likely to affect families with children, lone parents, families from specific ethnic minorities as well as families who have a child with a disability. Poverty affects the health and development of children and there is good evidence to suggest that children living in poverty lag behind in terms of educational achievement and are more likely to suffer from chronic diseases.

> Child poverty blights childhoods. Growing up in poverty means being cold, going hungry, not being able to join in activities with friends. For example, 61 per cent of families in the bottom income quintile would like, but cannot afford, to take their children on holiday for one week a year. Child poverty has long-lasting effects. By 16, children receiving free school meals achieve 1.7 grades lower at GCSE than their wealthier peers. Leaving school with fewer qualifications translates into lower earnings over the course of a working life.
>
> *CPAG, 2013*

Poverty also impacts on communities which mean there are fewer resources available for children and families and housing quality is poorer. Whilst not all children living in poverty can be defined as children in need, it is clear that poverty exacerbates needs and impacts on parents' and carers' ability to provide for and promote the welfare of their children. The increasing number of food banks in the UK suggests that families including working families are struggling to provide sufficient food for their children and they are making choices between heating their home and providing food as fuel poverty increases (BBC, 2013; Trussell Trust, 2013). Similarly, housing and homelessness organizations, such as Shelter, report that an increased number of families are at risk of losing their homes, or being moved into temporary accommodation, thus disrupting their children's education and severing established and reciprocal support and friendship networks (Shelter, 2013). Universal services are often not equipped to address the complex issues that living in poverty raises and the problem it throws up for families already struggling to cope. As financial and housing problems increase, many more children are likely to move into a category of need that they were never intended to occupy, putting a strain on already stretched statutory services.

Children in need of support: multiply disadvantaged

This book draws on key examples from case law which illustrate the application and legal deliberations which have informed statutory social work practice with children in need and their families. Key cases, legal and practice issues are then discussed in chapters about specific groups of children in need of support including: separated, unaccompanied and refugee children; children with disabilities; **care leavers**; and children with harmful sexual behaviour. These groups of children in need were identified for several reasons but principally because they are multiply disadvantaged.

There are real concerns about the treatment of migrant children coming to the UK (Crawley, 2012) and their needs being marginalized. The status of unaccompanied children raises issues about who has parental responsibility and who is responsible for their care and support needs. In recent years the appeal courts have responded with decisions which promote the rights and interests of migrant children and have been critical of local authorities who have attempted to evade their duties, particularly towards unaccompanied children. These decisions have a bearing on all unaccompanied children and social workers need to be aware of the implications of these decisions when assessing the needs of unaccompanied and asylum-seeking children and when identifying and providing services.

Children with disabilities are defined as children in need in s. 17(10)(c) Children Act 1989. Many families are managing the care of children with very complex disabilities and rely on social workers and other child and social/health care practitioners to provide advice and assistance. This advice is particularly important when health and care needs have to be distinguished for funding, around times of transition and in terms of access to education. Increasing numbers of children with complex disabilities are surviving into adulthood and social workers' knowledge of the legislation and practice in this area is crucial to ensure that the rights of these children are promoted and that they have access to advocacy when decisions are being made about them.

When they leave care, young people move into adulthood, often with limited support and sometimes without the skills and knowledge that they need to negotiate access to housing, education and training. UK legislation recognizes this group as being in need of support and the age at which care leavers can continue to access support has been extended until they are 25 years old in certain cases. The multiple disadvantages experienced by care leavers and the impact of these into adulthood are well documented. The longer-term needs of care leavers for support are included in recent legislation and guidance and it is important that social workers are informed as to the support entitlements of the different groups of care leavers.

There are growing concerns that children and young people with harmful sexual behaviour are criminalized at the expense of meeting their need for support. These, like other children in need of support discussed in this book, are a diverse group and their need for support is explicit in the research. Developing practice responses which foreground their need for support as well as managing the risk they may present requires a sensitive approach which situates them first and foremost as children in need.

In short these groups of children are multiply vulnerable and their situations are often complex and will require social work intervention and support from a range of agencies who often rely on social workers' knowledge of the legislation and practice guidance. Whilst there are undoubtedly many other children in need of support, the issues facing the children in this group are not straightforward and nor is their legal status. In addition, an economic climate which is characterized by deepening welfare benefit cuts and a rolling-back of the state threatens the already precarious situations for these children in need of support. There are two books in this series that focus on *Child Protection* (Holt, 2014) and *Looked After Children* (Ball, 2014) which readers are directed to as they deal more specifically with the legislation and practice guidance as it applies to these groups.

As well as discussing the range of legislation and policy which applies, this book highlights key examples of where and when to apply practice guidance and uses case examples to illustrate the process of assessment, intervention and review. Each chapter provides key points covered at the start, includes reference to additional sources which support the discussion of legislation and practice guidance, and suggests further reading to develop the knowledge and understanding of the issues covered.

Chapter outline

Chapter 1 of this book provides detail on the legal framework and the duties, powers and responsibilities which local authorities have in respect of children in need of support, and how the interpretation and application of the legislation in the guidance has informed practice. Chapter 2 covers assessment and the practice guidance which governs this, as well as outlining examples of community-based provisions which promote the welfare of children in need of support. Chapter 3 deals with children's rights and the relevance of the UNCRC and ECHR in domestic legislation. Chapters 4 to 7 focus on four specific groups of children and young people, and chapter 8 summarizes the key issues raised and concludes with some points for practice.

Chapter 1: The legal framework

This chapter introduces the legal framework for the provisions in the Children Act 1989, the **no order principle** and the provisions in the Children Act 2004. The provisions in Part III and specifically in s.17 Children Act 1989 are discussed and particularly the definition of children in need, and the duties which require local authorities to identify children in need and provide services.

Chapter 2: Children in need of support

In practice, cases where children come to the attention of statutory services have to meet the **threshold criteria** and resource gatekeeping distinguishes between those children who are prioritized as they may be at risk of *significant harm*, and those who require assessment because they meet the *children in need* criteria. This chapter explores some of the practical steps and approaches which are used in assessing children in need, drawing on the *Framework for Assessment of Children in Need and their Families* (Department of Health (DH), 2000) and *Working Together to Safeguard Children* (HM Government, 2013) – the practice guidance which now informs assessment practice. Many children in need of support will not require statutory intervention under s.17 Children Act 1989, however, community and family support mechanisms require resourcing and the local authority duty under s. 17(1)(b) in this respect is discussed here.

This chapter also looks at several models of early intervention practice which support children and their families in an effort to keep them out of statutory services. Community-based and voluntary sector organizations are often more attractive to families with children in need of support as they are less stigmatizing and families have some degree of control over when and how they access these.

Chapter 3: Children in need and children's rights

Chapter 3 discusses the Human Rights Act 1998 (HRA) and the UNCRC and illustrates how these international conventions inform UK legislation. Cases which have come before the European Court and the UK courts illustrate just how important it is that social worker practice with children in need is informed by a rights perspective, particularly Article 8 European Convention on Human Rights (ECHR) in the HRA in terms of the right to family life. There are a number of articles in the UNCRC which directly relate to the groups of children in need discussed in this book. The provisions in s. 17(4) Children Act 1989 and subsequent legislation place a duty on local authorities to ensure that children are part of any decision-making process which concerns them and that due weight is given to their **wishes and feelings**. However, there are tensions in this as children in need are often excluded from being party to decisions made about their welfare. Their participation (Article 12 ECHR) and their best interests (Article 3 ECHR) are two areas where the interests of children are often superseded. The difficulties in aligning practice with children's rights perspectives are discussed in this chapter as well as the concerns raised by the UN Monitoring Committee about the UK's record on promoting the rights of the children who are the subject of discussion in this book.

Chapter 4: Separated, unaccompanied and refugee children

Chapter 4 examines how the legislation informs social work intervention and assessment with separated, unaccompanied and asylum-seeking children. The provisions within the Children Act 1989 determine that children arriving in the UK unaccompanied are children in need. However, UK entry regulations and wider concerns about immigration tend to seep into debates about the needs of unaccompanied children and affect their entitlement to services. This is also a concern for refugee children who come to the UK with their families, particularly when they have exhausted the appeal process and have no recourse to public funds.

The support needs of unaccompanied children may differ from other groups of children in need, but their needs for stability and security are clear. The assessment process regarding unaccompanied children is further complicated by the additional requirements for **age assessment** to determine their eligibility for support. The difficulties facing separated and unaccompanied children, promoting their best interests and ensuring that they can return to their country of origin if it is in their best interests, and if they wish to do so, are a constant tension which social work practice has to balance. The legislation and practice guidance offers much advice on how best to accomplish this and appeal court rulings make the legal position very clear in many instances.

Chapter 5: Children with disabilities

Chapter 5 considers the assessment and support needs of children with disabilities. As with other groups of children in need, children with disabilities require ongoing assessment and regular review principally because of the changing and evolving nature of many disabilities and the impact on their health and development. Children with disabilities are often reliant on their parents and carers into their adulthood and transitions between child and adult services can be fraught with difficulties as services and resources may no longer be appropriate. The personalization agenda has also introduced choice and enablement more effectively into the support systems for families of children with disabilities. The courts have made several rulings in relation to the care and treatment of children with disabilities specifically children who may have deteriorating conditions. In addition the type, level and access to support for carers is laid out in several Acts which recognize the important work which carers do and the assistance they need to continue caring. This is especially true in the case of mothers. Respite care, education, access to leisure and play opportunities and independence are all areas of focus in this chapter.

Chapter 6: Young people leaving care

Chapter 6 considers the range of issues related to young people who are care leavers. The principles of the legislation provide for these young people to have access to support into adulthood, recognizing that the transition period from care to independence is challenging for care leavers, their carers and families. In addition it is now accepted and understood that leaving care is a process and not a single event. The legislation and practice guidance now defines who is a care leaver and provides for children and young people who have had had different levels of involvement in the care system, including unaccompanied children who come to the UK and have been looked after by local authorities. Research about care leavers suggests that they are a vulnerable group and have poorer outcomes on several important measures of well-being.

Social work practice in this area requires an understanding of the role of the **personal advisor** and the various stages of **transition planning** using the **pathway plan** as a guide as well as the eligibility criteria which apply to different care leavers.

Chapter 7: Children who display harmful sexual behaviour

Chapter 7 discusses the needs of children who have displayed harmful sexual behaviour. This group of children may be overlooked in practice as they are considered perpetrators and there is, of course, a risk that such children are treated by the law as criminals and sex offenders, whilst their needs as children are disregarded. However, the research suggests that children who display harmful sexual behaviour and who sexually abuse or assault other children have often been the victims of abuse and/or neglect themselves, and a significant proportion have learning disabilities and thus may have a range of unmet needs. The key issues in social work assessment and intervention relate to the management of risk and ensuring parents and/or carers understand how best to support these children. Specialist training for workers and carers and the availability of therapeutic interventions are crucial to addressing the harmful sexual behaviour.

Chapter 8: Conclusions

The final chapter in this book draws together and summarizes the discussions of these groups of children and outlines the approaches to practice which social work practitioners are required to adopt in order to ensure they are fulfilling their obligations and duties to assess, review and provide services to meet the needs of these children.

Further reading

Davies, M (ed.) *(2012) Social Work with Children and Families*: this comprehensive edited textbook covers a wide range of practice-related aspects of social work and, as well as discussing practice examples, each section draws on theory, legislation and research.

Montgomery, H and M Kellett (eds) (2009) *Children and Young People's Worlds: Developing Frameworks for Integrated Practice*: this edited collection provides a range of critical perspectives about the condition of childhood and the local and global contemporary issues which affect and shape children and young people's lives.

1
THE LEGAL FRAMEWORK

AT A GLANCE THIS CHAPTER COVERS:

- the statutory provisions in Children Act 1989
- section 17 Children Act 1989
- Children Act 2004 provisions
- local authority s. 17 duties and powers
- legal tensions
- *Framework for the Assessment of Children in Need and their Families*

Part I Children Act 1989 starts from the premise that the welfare of children is paramount and cases should only come to court where no other alternative is available. Implicit within the Act is the notion that early intervention can prevent longer-term impact on children's development and reduce the likelihood of children being removed from the care of their parents. Part III Children Act 1989 instituted the concept of *children in need* and made provision for their support at local authority level. This chapter discusses the evolving nature of the concept of children in need and also examines how local authorities might and do interpret their duties towards children in need in their area. The difficulties and challenges in assessing and providing support to children in need are discussed drawing on recent research, on case-specific examination, and issues related to quality in assessment practice.

Hendrick (1994) examines the way in which child care social work came under significant public and political scrutiny during the 1980s following a series of very high-profile child deaths – including Jasmine Beckford, Heidi Koseda and Tyra Henry in 1984, Kimberley Carlisle in 1986, and Doreen Mason in 1987. In all of these cases the children were known to social workers. The inquiries following their deaths at the hands of their parents and step-parents levelled harsh criticism at the local authorities and the National Society for the Prevention of Cruelty to Children (NSPCC) for failing to take sufficient action to protect the children. Conversely, the public enquiry into the Cleveland affair in 1987 (Butler-Sloss, 1988) criticized the intrusive activities of social workers who removed children from their parents. Dozens of children were subjected to questionable and controversial diagnosis of sexual abuse by a hospital paediatrician. Not only had workers acted in haste, they had also excluded parents, using 'place of safety' orders to remove children in what was deemed to be a traumatic manner. The Children Act 1989 was thus designed to strike a better balance between parents and the state and introduced new concepts which emphasized partnership between parents and the state, parental responsibility and support for children and families. There was a shift away from the state (via the courts) being involved in family life and the introduction of local authority duties and powers to support children and families in s. 17.

Key principles of the Children Act 1989

The key principles of the Children Act 1989 were designed to ensure that children and their best interests were prioritized in decision-making about them. A balance was required to ensure that those cases coming to court were only the most complex that could not be dealt with by other formal community-based mechanisms. These principles determine that the welfare of children is paramount in any proceedings about them. Section 1 states that:

s. 1

(1) When a court determines any question with respect to:
   (a) the upbringing of a child; or
   (b) the administration of a child's property or the application of any income arising from it, the child's welfare shall be the court's paramount consideration.
(2) In any proceedings in which any question with respect to the upbringing of a child arises, the court shall have regard to the general principle that any delay in determining the question is likely to prejudice the welfare of the child.
(3) In the circumstances mentioned in subsection (4), a court shall have regard in particular to—
   (a) the ascertainable wishes and feelings of the child concerned (considered in the light of his age and understanding);
   (b) his physical, emotional and educational needs;
   (c) the likely effect on him of any change in his circumstances;
   (d) his age, sex, background and any characteristics of his which the court considers relevant;
   (e) any harm which he has suffered or is at risk of suffering;
   (f) how capable each of his parents, and any other person in relation to whom the court considers the question to be relevant, is of meeting his needs;
   (g) the range of powers available to the court under this Act in the proceedings in question.
(4) The circumstances are that—
   (a) the court is considering whether to make, vary or discharge a section 8 order, and the making, variation or discharge of the order is opposed by any party to the proceedings; or
   (b) the court is considering whether to make, vary or discharge a special guardianship order or an order under Part IV.

Children Act 1989

Cases about children should only be brought before the courts when other options have been tried. In an important step forward the Children Act 1989 formalized the requirement for children's wishes and feelings to be heard and introduced the 'no order' principle. This s. 1(5) principle was designed to prevent cases coming to the courts if it was better not to make an order:

s. 1(5)

> Where a court is considering whether or not to make one or more orders under this Act with respect to a child, it shall not make the order or any of the orders unless it considers that doing so would be better for the child than making no order at all.
>
> *Children Act 1989*

In s. 2 the concept of parental responsibility as a formal status is introduced and defined in s. 3, whilst s. 4 determines who can have parental responsibility and how it is acquired. Where parents are married they each have parental responsibility.

Unmarried fathers can acquire parental responsibility in a number of ways: s. 4 Children Act 1989 deals with the acquisition of parental responsibility by a child's father:

s. 4

(1) Where a child's father and mother were not married to each other at the time of his birth the father shall acquire parental responsibility for the child if—
   - (a) he becomes registered as the child's father under any of the enactments specified in subsection (1A);
   - (b) he and the child's mother make an agreement (a 'parental responsibility agreement') providing for him to have parental responsibility for the child; or
   - (c) the court, on his application, orders that he shall have parental responsibility for the child.

Children Act 1989

This was amended in s. 111(1) and (3) Adoption and Children Act 2002.

Step-parents and others who might care for a child are also able to acquire parental responsibility. It was expected that the implementation of the Children Act 1989 would divert cases away from the courts and it was recognized that alternative community-based provisions would be required to provide support to families and children.

Statutory provisions in the Children Act 1989

Part III Children Act 1989 includes the statutory provisions for local authority support for children and families. Section 17(1) deals with the provision of services for children in need, their families and others:

s. 17(1)

> It shall be the general duty of every local authority ...
> (a) to safeguard and promote the welfare of children within their area who are in need; and
> (b) so far as is consistent with that duty, to promote the upbringing of such children by their families, by providing a range and level of services appropriate to those children's needs.
>
> *Children Act 1989*

The Children Act 1989 shifted the focus towards supporting families with children, and ensuring the safety and well-being of children. As well as emphasizing that parents have primary responsibility for their children, local authorities are required to support parents and families and provide services to enable families to support the welfare of their children.

The definition of a child in need

Children in need are defined broadly in **s.** 17(10) Children Act 1989:

s. 17(10)

> For the purposes of this Part a child shall be taken to be in need if
> (a) he is unlikely to achieve or maintain, or to have the opportunity of achieving or maintaining, a reasonable standard of health or development without the provision for him of services by a local authority under this Part;
> (b) his health or development is likely to be significantly impaired, or further impaired, without the provision for him of such services; or
> (c) he is disabled,
> and 'family', in relation to such a child, includes any person who has parental responsibility for the child and any other person with whom he has been living.
>
> *Children Act 1989*

The extension to every child who has disabilities was welcomed as a step in the right direction as it was designed to alter the way in which local authorities engaged with children and their families and was intended to ensure that standards of care, support, protection and review of needs were appropriate to the needs of children with disabilities and their families. However, as the cases discussed in this book illustrate, local authorities throughout the UK challenge their duties to provide support to children in need, and restrict through gatekeeping and assessment processes access to statutory services and support.

Jordan (2012) discusses the difference in definitions of children in need that families have and the legal definition and suggests that often families understand 'in need' to mean that, without extra support services, their child's health, development or well-being will be affected as they will be denied the advantages that additional local authority support could bring. However, the local authority can make decisions about how to exercise its duties by the determination of what is meant by 'reasonable standard' (s. 17(10)(a) Children Act 1989) and 'significantly impaired' (s. 17(10)(b)). In effect, professional judgments are made based on the interpretations of these two words ('in need') by professionals and in accordance with these definitions.

The definitions of health and development are the same definitions used in s. 31 Children Act 1989 and the application of criteria to determine whether care proceedings are necessary. The relationship between a child requiring protection and a child being in need is based on a child in need–child protection continuum and the professional judgment by the social worker which informs the assessment of whether or not the needs can be met by the child's parents/carers. A general principle is that children in need are those whose needs cannot be met through universal education and health services. Of course, there are difficulties in ensuring that all parties agree on what services might be provided.

Identifying and supporting children in need

As well as identifying children in need within their area and ensuring a range of services are available to meet these needs, local authorities are required to undertake assessments, provide family support services and resources and take steps to prevent the accommodation of children and care proceedings. This general duty does not, however, mean that individual children have universal rights to support. Instead, the local authority has a duty to identify children in need and provide services to support them in their families. As the cases in the previous section illustrate, the reality is that services for children in need are targeted or rationed and this presents challenges for parents and professionals who must make the best use of the limited resources available and negotiate the tensions between agencies commissioned to provide services and allocate services to families.

Local authorities must also act lawfully in their decision-making and rationing of resources for children in need. Schedule 2 Children Act 1989 outlines the requirements for local authority support to all children and families. This includes:

- identification of children in need and provision of information;
- maintenance of a register of disabled children;
- assessment of children's needs;
- prevention of neglect and abuse;
- provision of accommodation in order to protect child;
- provision for disabled children (amended by Children and Young Persons Act 2008);
- provision to reduce need for care proceedings etc.;
- provision for children living with their families;
- provision for accommodated children (amended by Children and Young Persons Act 2008);
- maintenance of the family home;
- duty to consider racial groups to which children in need belong.

Section 17(10) Children Act 1989 laid out the expectation that local authorities would identify children in their locality whose health and development are being compromised by their individual or family circumstances. The local authority must determine what those needs are, and ensure that appropriate and relevant services are available either by directly providing them or commissioning them from voluntary or private sector organizations. Section 10 Children Act 2004 made provision for the cooperation of relevant and specific agencies in local authorities to promote the well-being of children and young people in their area. In doing so the legislation reaffirmed a commitment to working with parents (s. 10(3)), and ensuring the availability of adequate and appropriate resources and pooled funds (s. 10(6)).

Section 17 duties of the local authority

Section 17 Children Act 1989 is a general duty conferred on local authorities which have a number of duties to provide services for the welfare of children with an emphasis on preventative support and services for families. In addition, s. 17 drew a distinction between all children in need and those defined as 'in need'. However, as discussed, this also suggests that resource pressure may lead to only the neediest of those at risk being provided with services and this is a constant challenge which practitioners and managers find themselves dealing with.

Under Part III Children Act 1989 local authorities have a duty to provide support for children in need and their families. Family is defined for this purpose as parents and children, as well as any person with parental responsibility or any other person with whom the child is living (s. 17(10)). Services are to be provided if they are going to safeguard or promote the welfare of a child in need (s. 17 (3). Part III also includes duties related to the provision of services (ss 17–19) and the provision of accommodation (ss 20 and 21) as well as duties towards children who are looked after.

These duties of local authorities are defined in s. 17(1) Children Act 1989:

s. 17(1)

It shall be the general duty of every local authority:

(a) to safeguard and promote the welfare of children within their area who are in need; and

(b) so far as is consistent with that duty, to promote the upbringing of such children by their families.

Children Act 1989

There are also now specific obligations to ensure a sufficient supply of certain services for disabled children, for instance, childcare; under s. 6(5) Childcare Act 2006. The duty on local authorities to secure sufficient childcare for working parents applies in relation to disabled children up to the age of 18.

In s. 17(10) Children Act 1989, a child shall be taken to be in need if:

s. 17(10)

(a) he is unlikely to achieve or maintain, or to have the opportunity of achieving or maintaining, a reasonable standard of health or development without the provision for him of services by a local authority under this Part;

(b) his health or development is likely to be significantly impaired, or further impaired, without the provision for him of such services; or

(c) he is disabled,

and 'family', in relation to such a child, includes any person who has parental responsibility for the child and any other person with whom he has been living.

Children Act 1989

In s. 17(11) a disabled child is defined as in the definition included in s. 29(1) National Assistance Act 1948: 'persons who are blind, deaf or dumb, and other persons who are substantially permanently handicapped by illness, injury, or congenital deformity or such other disabilities'.

Legal entitlements

Wise et al. (2011) offer a stark warning to local authorities who evade their duties which are:

> ... clear and enforceable and it is no exaggeration to suggest that downgrading these duties to mere discretionary powers undermines the rule of law ... it does not matter how the child comes to be in need of support, what matters is that if a child is, for whatever reason, in need of support, such support as is needed should be provided.
>
> *Wise et al., 2011:6–7*

The entitlements of children in need are as follows.

Participation and best interests

They must be allowed, where it is reasonably practicable, to participate in any decisions taken about their lives (s. 17(4A)(b)). Decisions must give their best interests primary consideration and respect their rights to family and private life.

Assessment

They are able to have an independent determination of **age** if this is **disputed** by the state. They are entitled to an initial assessment and if it is considered that support may be needed from several agencies then a core assessment must be offered.

Services and support

Children in need are entitled to:

- services to meet their assessed needs where the conditions in one of the statutory duties are met or where intervention is required;
- a care plan which should be a realistic plan of action;
- suitable accommodation where parents or carers are prevented from providing them with suitable care or accommodation;
- support as a 'looked after' child if they are accommodated for more than 24 hours;
- a personal advisor and a pathway plan after the age of 16 if they are a care leaver;
- legal aid to challenge any failure to realize these entitlements.

Even if a public body only has a power and not a duty to confer a particular benefit on a child or their family so that no entitlement to the benefit arises, that power still has to be exercised rationally, reasonably and fairly. There has to be a transparent and equitable decision-making process. This is important because, in the current economic context of dwindling public resources and already over-stretched local authorities, the decision related to the local authority exercising powers may be seen as a reduction or withdrawal of services. There is also the potential or likelihood of cases coming to the appeal courts and judicial review if those decisions are found not to have been made fairly or rationally. In addition, as was found in Laming (2003), the inquiry into the death of Victoria Climbié, the London Boroughs of Ealing, Brent and Haringey were:

> … at the time of Victoria's case, all spending significantly below their Standard Spending Assessment (SSA) on services for children. This was in sharp contrast with the national picture, where most local authorities were overspending their SSA on services for children and families. (Laming 2003:14)

It is thus crucial that social workers undertaking assessments, service managers, council officials and elected members who allocate resources are fully informed as to the powers and duties of their authorities in respect of children in need.

| *On-the-spot question* | What non-legal factors might influence your assessment of whether or not a child is in need? |

Once a referral is made to children's social care, an initial assessment will determine whether or not a child is defined as 'in need'. Several questions will assist in the decision-making process here:

- How does the child meet the 'child in need' criteria for an assessment?
- Is the child a child in need as per s. 17 Children Act 1989?
- Is this authority the authority that has a duty to assess and provide services?
- If the child is 'in need' will that child be eligible to other services as a result of being 'in need'?
- Should a child 'in need' be placed with its family?
- Does the child meet the threshold for an assessment as a child in need or are there concerns about significant harm which may warrant a child protection investigation (s. 47)?

> **KEY CASE ANALYSIS**

R (on the Application of OO) v London Borough Of Hackney [2013]

The question of whether a child is in need is dependent upon the outcomes of an assessment. The quality of the assessment in this case was thought to be poor and, although the judge agreed that the quality of the assessment was lacking, the outcome of the assessment was accepted.

The mother of three children claimed that her children were 'in need' and, despite the solicitor for OO criticizing the assessments which had been undertaken, the judge declined a judicial review on the grounds that the local authority had looked at the case fairly and come to the correct decision. The reports from the children's school suggested that they were well cared for and enjoyed a close, loving relationship with their mother OO. This was in sharp contrast to the claims made by OO that she was destitute and unable to provide for her children's welfare. In this case the judgment decided that the children were not *in need* and that the assessments which had been undertaken were appropriate. Indeed, OO had not always cooperated with social services and her case claiming that she was destitute and homeless was not accepted. The assessment information identified that OO had sufficient and extensive support networks. It is clear that it is not sufficient to simply criticize the assessment. In the case of OO the judge concluded that the assessment had been carried out fairly, the duty to assess had been met and the decision not to provide services was based on the assessment.

The children did meet the criteria for assessment but the assessment concluded that they were not *in need* as not only were there sufficient familial resources, there was also evidence contained in the assessment that the children were well cared for and not destitute. What this case also highlights is that entitlement to an assessment does not necessarily lead to the provision of services. The needs have to be sufficient to meet the s. 17(10) Children Act 1989 criteria.

On-the-spot question

If the assessment had identified that the children were in need, what duties would apply to provide services?

The child was assessed as being in need in this next case, however, the local authority declined to provide services on the grounds that the child was not ordinarily resident in the area for part of the year.

> **KEY CASE ANALYSIS** ←

R (on the Application of J) v Worcestershire County Council [2013]

In this case, the issue of whether the local authority should provide services came before the courts. The claimant was a three-year-old boy who suffered Down's syndrome and other complex medical problems, with developmental delay. His parents were of Romany Gypsy ethnicity and were fairground travellers. The paternal grandfather was retired and lived in a dwelling at a fixed address in the defendant local authority's area. The claimant and his family normally resided there during the winter break, still living in their caravan, but parking it on the grandfather's land. The authority agreed that the claimant was a child in need for the purpose of s. 17 Children Act 1989, but determined that it was not able or lacked power to provide any help or support whenever the claimant was outside its area, however briefly. The claimant sought judicial review of the authority's decision. He contended that the authority had misdirected itself as to the geographical reach or extent of its powers under s. 17 of the Act and sought a declaration that the authority's power to provide services under s. 17 of the Act applied to services that might be provided to the claimant when he was outside its area. The application was allowed because the local authority had a duty to assess and provide services even when the child was out of its area. The law was intended to ensure that the power to provide services was extended to when the child was not in the area as long as he remained a child in need.

> **On-the-spot question**
>
> What measures might need to be considered to work with this family given that for part of the year the child may not reside in the local authority's area which has a duty to provide services?

Cases have also been brought before the courts and the courts have found that local authorities have met their duties to provide for the child but not the support which is requested by the parent as in the following case.

⟶ **KEY CASE ANALYSIS** ⟵

R v London Borough of Barnet (Respondents) ex parte G (FC) (Appellant) [2003]

G, a Dutch national of Somali origin, was not eligible for housing assistance. She has a son, born in May 1999. G claimed she left The Netherlands because of social ostracism encountered there in the Somali community on account of her child's illegitimacy, and that she came to the UK to look for the child's father. G did not satisfy the habitual residence test and so an application to the London Borough of Barnet for assistance with housing was refused. G then sought assistance from Barnet Council, as the local social services authority, which assessed that the child's needs would be best met by the return of the child to Holland with G the mother as they would be immediately entitled to accommodation and other benefits. The council did not accept the mother's account of her reasons for coming to London. G applied for judicial review of this decision and argued that it was not in her child's best interests to be removed from her care which would happen unless she was housed and able to access benefits. If the mother refused to return to The Netherlands, the council intended to place the child with foster parents, and to provide no accommodation for the mother. Interim relief was granted in the judicial review proceedings. The decision was later quashed. The child was in need, and it was in the best interests of the child to live with his mother. Given the duties imposed on the local authority by s. 17(1) Children Act 1989, and the powers granted to it by s. 23, the local authority 'has no alternative' but to place the child with his mother, assuming it is reasonably practicable to do so. This was so even though the mother was, in the view of the local authority, acting unreasonably. The council duly appealed and the judicial review application was dismissed. The judge said the duty imposed by

s. 17(1) was met by providing financial assistance for the return of the mother and child to Holland. The local authority did not act unlawfully in refusing to provide assistance in cash or in kind to assist in the provision of accommodation for the mother and her child. Section 17(3) and (6) imposed no such duty on the local authority. Section 20 imposed a duty to provide accommodation for the child, not for the parent and the child.

This case illustrates that the assessment of the local authority and its decision that to provide assistance for return and not for accommodation was not unlawful was accepted by the court. In this case, it was accepted that the child was in need but the local authority made a different assessment of what was in the child's best interests. It agreed to fund return journeys for the child and mother, but not to provide accommodation to meet the needs of the child.

In another case, *R (on the Application of G) v Southwark London Borough Council* [2009], the court had to decide if the local authority had acted lawfully in assessing that the claimant was a child in need (s. 17) and entitled to support when the claimant argued that he should be provided with accommodation under s. 20 Children Act 1989 which covers the provision of accommodation for children:

s. 20

(1) Every local authority shall provide accommodation for any child in need within their area who appears to them to require accommodation as a result of:
  (a) there being no person who has parental responsibility for him;
  (b) his being lost or having been abandoned; or
  (c) the person who has been caring for him being prevented (whether or not permanently, and for whatever reason) from providing him with suitable accommodation or care.

Children Act 1989

The claimant came to the UK with his mother and siblings in 1998. He was granted indefinite leave to remain in 2005. Relations with his mother deteriorated and he left his family home. He approached the local housing authority, which unsuccessfully attempted mediation. After staying with friends, the claimant, aged 17, consulted solicitors who advised him to present himself to social services and request an assessment of his needs under s. 17 Children Act 1989, and immediate accommodation under s. 20(1) of that Act. The claimant was given temporary bed-and-breakfast accommodation pending the authority's investigation. The initial assessment was completed and the report concluded that there were not additional needs or vulnerabilities that would suggest the need for longer-term accommodation being provided by social services. He was not in full-time education at this point in time, therefore the accommodation provided by the authority's homeless persons unit and referrals to other support agencies was deemed sufficient to work on addressing the social, emotional and practical issues identified in his assessment. The report also referred the claimant to the authority's own family resource team, which could provide:

- social work support;
- help him in dealings with the Department for Work and Pensions in applying for benefits;
- explore holding a family group conference to work on reconciling him with his mother;
- link in with his prospective college and provide any support necessary for his enrolment;
- and referral to an agency giving housing and careers advice.

The authority maintained that s. 20 Children Act 1989 was not the appropriate section in the instant case and that it had fulfilled its duty to the claimant who was not an unaccompanied minor. It had carried out an assessment and identified support for the claimant as above. The claimant unsuccessfully sought judicial review of that decision. The Court of Appeal dismissed the claimant's appeal, finding that the authority had been entitled to conclude that he had required only 'help with accommodation' under s. 17 Children Act 1989 and not accommodation under s. 20(1).

In *R v London Borough of Lambeth (Respondents) ex parte W (FC) (Appellant)* [2003], the issue was about housing and whether the local authority should provide accommodation to the family or simply to the children whilst the mother found alternative accommodation. W, who had two children aged 16 and 7, had become intentionally homeless within the meaning of that expression in the homelessness legislation and sought assistance for accommodation from the London Borough of Lambeth as the local social services authority. This was refused. In a further assessment Lambeth Council decided it should explore placing the children with extended family members in the short term whilst the mother sought alternative accommodation. This provision could be made for the children alone under s. 20 Children Act 1989. The Court of Appeal dismissed an appeal in respect of the council's decision and considered there were not sufficient grounds for interfering with the council's decision. The court held that s. 17 Children Act 1989 imposes a duty on the council in respect of services to children in need, but not in relation to individual children – where the council only has a power. The council had provided clear reasons as to why it was not willing to exercise its power in this case, balancing other pressures on its resources. As such, where all else failed the local authority has power to help under s. 17, but it can reserve this power for extreme cases which this case was not deemed to be.

In these appeal court cases the duty owed by the local authority to an individual child or family was limited and the child in need does not have a right to the services even when assessed. The second issue in these cases related to the view of the appeal court that the local authority had some degree of discretion and was able to make judgments in light of the availability of resources it could and was able to provide or commission for children in need.

This chapter has discussed the development of 'in need' as a legal concept introduced in s. 17 Children Act 1989. The tensions in what families define as 'in need' in respect of their own children and what duties and powers local authorities have in regard to children in need and their families were explored. As discussed, local authorities can exercise some discretion in terms of their powers but not in a way which undermines the rule of law.

Further reading

DH (2000) *Framework for the Assessment of Children in Need and their Families.* Although this has now been replaced by *Working Together* (DfE, 2013c), this document remains a rich source of information about the processes involved in the assessment as well as containing clear references to theories and approaches which underpin assessment work with children and their families.

Hendrick, H (1994) *Child Welfare: England 1872–1989.* Hendrick's now classic work examines the history of legislation, ideology and theory related to child welfare policies and practice. Chapter 11 of this book discusses the development of the Children Act 1989 against a backdrop of the public inquiries in the 1970s and 1980s.

Holland, S (2011) *Child and Family Assessment in Social Work*. Holland usefully outlines the processes of assessment and discusses some of the fundamental issues related to undertaking an assessment as a legalistic task.

Jordan, L (2012) 'The legal foundations of family support work' in M Davies (ed.), *Social Work with Children and Families*. This chapter examines the legal basis for how the range of family support for children in need is defined and lays out the key issues for social workers.

2

CHILDREN IN NEED OF SUPPORT

In some circumstances family problems and issues, such as housing, homelessness and family breakdown, lead to children being in need and this large group of children often remains hidden in official statistics until their needs escalate and they require statutory safeguarding intervention, for example, the s. 47 Children Act 1989 duty to investigate risk of significant harm. This chapter discusses assessments and the guidance which informs them. Because of the differences in how needs are understood and responded to, practice guidance stipulates what an assessment should cover. Local authority threshold criteria can often exclude children from accessing resources and services and so an understanding of the dimensions of need, potential avenues of support and close liaison with other agencies is important. The third (voluntary and community) sector plays an important role in promoting and developing community-based models of support to children in need which support families and work with them in partnership to address their needs outside of statutory services. These services can be provided under s. 17(1) Children Act 1989.

s. 17(1)

It shall be the general duty of every local authority

(a) to safeguard and promote the welfare of children within their area who are in need; and

(b) so far as is consistent with that duty, to promote the upbringing of such children by their families,

by providing a range and level of services appropriate to those children's needs.

Children Act 1989

Framework for the Assessment of Children in Need and their Families

The *Framework for the Assessment of Children in Need and their Families* was introduced in 2000 to address assessment deficits and concerns that there was too narrow a focus on incidents of maltreatment and immediate protection and not enough attention paid to a parent's ability to meet the specific needs of the child (DH, 2000). Socio-economic factors, for example, were minimized as was their impact on parenting issues and there was a lack of clarity amongst professionals regarding their roles (Horwath, 2011). The result of these shortfalls in the assessment was a real lack of focus on the needs of individual children which the assessment framework was designed to address. The assessment framework draws from many disciplines, research and practice experience about the developmental needs of children. Included in the guidance is recognition that many families are parenting under stress and that families have a right to expect practical support from universal services, such as health and education. The guidance accepts that families experience difficulties from time to time for a range of reasons and these may impact on their children: the death of a family member; physical or mental ill health; divorce or parental separation or sudden loss of employment; multiple births, or having a child with disabilities or special educational needs (SEN). In addition it is also recognized in the guidance that not all adults are prepared for the stress and daily rigours of parenting and that particular stages of childhood are difficult to cope with: 'Many cope well enough with one problem but a combination of problems can have a cumulative debilitating effect.' (DH, 2000:2)

Many families who are dealing with difficult circumstances receive support from their family and friends as well as from universal and community-based services. This can enable them to deal with problems. These families will not require additional support services. Belsky and Vondra (1989, cited in DH, 2000:2) describe parenting as 'a buffered system'. However, limited access to or a lack of family and community resources may impact on the welfare of the child and, in these cases, additional support is needed. This may include services which parents pay for, such as day care, or services provided by the local authority or by voluntary sector organizations. For some families, targeted support will be required. The guidance accepts that families seeking help from social services have different levels of need and, for many, help, advice or the provision of short-term practical services will be sufficient. However, for a smaller number of families who have serious and complex problems, a detailed assessment which may involve other agencies in that process will be required to develop and implement an appropriate intervention. The *Framework for the Assessment of Children in Need* includes a wide range of child development research and theory to provide for practitioners working with children and their families a structured assessment tool based on three interrelated dimensions: child development, parenting capacity and family and environmental factors (DH, 2000:2).

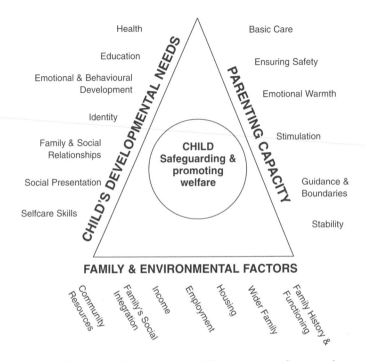

Figure 2.1: Diagram of the dimensions of the assessment framework
Source: Framework for the Assessment of Children in Need and their Families, DH, 2000:89

| On-the-spot question | What are the benefits of a structured assessment for children and families? |

The guidance for the assessment framework outlines the legislation, responsibilities and principles which underpin assessment work in local authority departments and health authorities in promoting and safeguarding children's welfare. It provides a detailed description of the framework and the assessment process. In the guidance there is reference to the needs of children in general and to children who may have specific needs and impairments. The roles and responsibilities of agencies involved in inter-agency assessment are discussed and the guidance refers to the organizational arrangements required to support effective assessment of children in need:

> ... local authorities corporately have a responsibility to address the needs of such children and young people. There should be effective joint working by education, housing and leisure in partnership with social services and health. Social services alone cannot promote the social inclusion and development of these children and families.
>
> *DH, 2000:64*

The framework refers to a wide range of agencies including: social services departments; voluntary and independent agencies; health authorities; the general practitioners and the primary health care team; nurses, midwives, health visitors and school nurses; paediatric services; professionals allied to health; mental health services; psychologists, education services; day-care services; Sure Start; Youth Offending Teams (YOTs); housing, the police; probation services; the prison service; and the armed services. All of these agencies may play a role in promoting the welfare of children in need.

> Individual practitioners will use their professional relationships and networks to assist them achieve good outcomes for children and their families. Quality collaboration at an inter-personal level requires effective organisational arrangements to support these informal processes and ensure good inter-agency working is not solely dependent on the commitment of dedicated individuals.
>
> *DH, 2000:79*

Whilst this guidance is now superseded by *Working Together to Safeguard Children* (2013) which came into force from 15 April 2013, ch. 2 of the guidance offers additional practice guidance on the individual dimensions of the three domains of assessment and can be referred to alongside *Working Together to Safeguard Children* (Department for Education (DfE), 2013c) to support the assessment process.

Working Together to Safeguard Children: A Guide to Interagency Working to Safeguard and Promote the Welfare of Children

This guidance covers the legislative requirements and expectations of individual services to safeguard and promote the welfare of children and provides a clear framework for LSCBs to monitor the effectiveness of local services. This guidance replaces *Working Together to Safeguard Children* (Department for Education and Skills (DfES), 2010); the *Framework for the Assessment of Children in Need and their Families* (DH, 2000); and statutory guidance on making arrangements to safeguard and promote the welfare of children under s. 11 Children Act 2004 (HM Government,

> **KEY CASE ANALYSIS**

R (on the Application of SJ and Another) v Surrey County Council [2014]

In this case the judge had to decide whether or not to allow an appeal which was brought before the court regarding whether or not the child was in need. The assessments which had been undertaken of SJ and her sibling LJ who lived with their aunt over a long period of time had different outcomes. In October 2010, an initial assessment of SJ and LJ concluded they did not constitute children in need within the meaning of the statutory definition. In April 2011, following a referral from JO, the relative looking after the children, the initial assessment concluded that each child was a child in need and financial assistance was provided in the form of food vouchers and, in October 2011, a core assessment was carried out. In November 2011, the judicial review application was made on the grounds that the children should have been treated under s. 20 Children Act 1989 for accommodation and the second aspect that, as children in need, the local authority support was inadequate. Interim relief was sought that the defendants should pay the national minimum foster care allowance rate to JO to support the children.

In this case the issues brought to the appeal court were in regard to the financial support which was made to the aunt. The subsequent assessments of LJ found that she was not a child in need, she had financial support from her school and from her father, as well as access to counselling services if she wished to use them. In effect the judge identified that what LJ was requesting were wants rather than needs and these wants had to be prioritized by the carer rather than presented as needs which had to be met by the state.

The main issue for determination was whether the local authority failure to treat SJ as a child in need within the meaning of s. 17 Children Act 1989 is outside the range of reasonable responses which are open to it or tainted by apparent bias. The judge dealt with each claim of bias in turn and found that, contrary to the claims by LJ, the local authority devoted great efforts and resources to support the family and had strived to fulfil its duties under difficult circumstances and numerous demands on limited resources.

2007). This is statutory guidance issued under s. 7 of the Local Authority Social Services Act 1970 (LASSA), which requires local authorities in their social services functions to act under the general guidance of the Secretary of State (s. 11(4) and s. 16 Children Act 2004).

The guidance states that, once identified, children in need may be assessed under s. 17 Children Act 1989, in relation to their SEN, disabilities, because they are a carer, or because they have committed a crime. The process for assessment should also be used for children whose parents are in prison and for asylum-seeking children. When assessing children in need and providing services, specialist assessments may be required and, where possible, should be coordinated so that the child and family experience a coherent process and a single plan of action (DfE, 2013c).

Whatever legislation the child is assessed under, the purpose of the assessment is always:

- to gather important information about a child and family;
- to analyse their needs and/or the nature and level of any risk and harm being suffered by the child;
- to decide whether the child is a child in need (s. 17 Children Act 1989) and/or is suffering or likely to suffer significant harm (s. 47 Children Act 1989); and
- to provide support to address those needs to improve the child's outcomes to make them safe.

Threshold criteria and significant harm

If as a result of an initial assessment it is apparent that there are concerns about the well-being and safety of the child, then the child might meet the *threshold criteria* for a care or supervision order. Section 31 Children Act 1989 sets out the legal basis, or the 'threshold criteria' for a care or supervision order in respect of a particular child. This threshold criteria must be met in that *the child must be suffering, or likely to suffer, significant harm* and that *the harm or likelihood of harm must be attributable to one of the following*: a) *the care given to the child, or likely to be given if the order were not made, not being what it would be reasonable to expect a parent to give*; or b) *the child being beyond parental control*. The Children Act 1989 defines harm as 'ill-treatment or the impairment of health or development' and development means physical, intellectual, emotional, social or behavioural development. 'Health' means physical or mental health; and 'ill-treatment' includes sexual abuse and forms of ill-treatment which are not physical. Part II s. 120 Adoption and Children Act 2002 extended the definition of harm to 'impairment suffered by hearing or seeing the ill-treatment of another'. This extension was introduced as a result of evidence from child welfare experts and research which found that children who are exposed to or witness domestic violence are harmed.

An assessment using the *Framework for the Assessment of Children in Need and their Families* may still be undertaken (DH, 2000), but the likelihood is that a s. 47 Children Act 1989 child protection investigation would need to be initiated following the *Working Together* (DfE, 2013c) guidance. This guidance sets out how practitioners should conduct the assessment of children. There is variation in s. 17 child in need thresholds, since what is provided, and who is deemed eligible for the interventions and how they are assessed, is at the discretion of local authorities:

> the interpretation of what constitutes 'significant harm' seems to depend on individual and collective judgements and inevitably varies as a consequence (House of Commons Education Committee, 2012:57).

Assessment practice

The *Framework for the Assessment of Children in Need and their Families* (DH, 2000) was introduced to address assessment deficits. There were concerns that there was too narrow a focus on incidents of maltreatment and immediate protection and not enough attention paid to a parent's ability to meet the specific needs of the child; socio-economic factors were minimized as was their impact on parenting issues and there was a lack of clarity amongst professionals regarding their roles (Horwath, 2010). The result of these shortfalls in the assessment was a real lack of focus on the needs of individual children. The emphasis on assessment of children in need contained in the *Framework for Assessment* (DH, 2000) is on an holistic assessment approach which accounts for three specific dimensions: child's developmental needs, parenting capacity and environmental factors. Cleaver and Walker (2004) examined the impact of the assessment framework and argue that these assessment procedures are incident-focused and, as such, there are missed opportunities to adequately assess need and provide relevant and timely resources to families. The DH's research programme in this area found a lack of systematic recording, along with a failure to identify family problems or assess their impact, and a lack of planning for outcomes led to children's needs not being met (Cleaver and Walker, 2004).

More recently Turney et al. (2011) conducted research funded by the DfE to gain a better understanding of the relationship between the quality of assessments and outcomes for children in contact with children's social care services. The aim was to increase understanding of the importance of quality assessments being undertaken of children in need. The study found that how information is collected and analysed during an assessment has both a short and long-term impact on future planning and choice of interventions. In addition, local authority policies affect decisions about the type of assessment which should be undertaken:

> Significant decisions are made on the basis of social work and other professional assessments that affect outcomes for children in both the short and the long term. Yet we know from research studies, inquiries into child deaths and overviews of serious case reviews that assessment is complex and challenging. The evidence shows that on occasion, practice has fallen short of the standard required. Poor quality, incomplete or non-existent assessments have been of particular concern.
>
> *Turney et al., 2011:1*

This research identified a series of problem areas in assessment: differential thresholds; a failure to engage the child; inadequate information-gathering; limited critical analysis; and deficiencies in inter-professional working. The review identified the increasing range of knowledge and skills needed when undertaking assessments. It also highlighted factors that contribute to or inhibit effective practice and the production of high quality assessment. Good assessment matters and is key to effective intervention and to ensure good outcomes for children (Turney et al., 2011).

Partnership work with children in need of support and their families

Social workers, youth justice workers, youth workers, play workers, key workers, family support workers, health visitors, parenting practitioners, occupational therapists and care workers are amongst the range of practitioners from a wide range of backgrounds, paid and unpaid, who work with children in need. The most important people, of course, are parents, who provide care and support for their children. Developing and sustaining relationships between parents and professionals is a key aspect of work with children in need and their families and throughout the assessment period and afterwards (Holland, 2011). The role of parents as partners in the provision of care for their children throughout childhood and into adulthood is crucial. Parents retain parental responsibility for their child through any children in need intervention and it is only in adoption cases that parental responsibility is lost.

> ... the assessment should be undertaken with the agreement of the child and their parents or carers. It should involve the child and family as well as all the professionals who are working with them (HM Government, 2013:12).

Whilst the new guidance as cited above does not explicitly state that social work assessments should be conducted in partnership with parents, effective practice requires this. Partnership with parents applies to the processes involved in all aspects of assessment work with families and is prioritized by social workers who see the positive consequences of working in this way in terms of better outcomes for children (Cleaver and Walker, 2004). This partnership should include explanations to the family about what is happening and why an assessment is being undertaken. Families also need to know what the process of assessment will involve and what the outcome of the assessment will be once it is in progress. Research evidence, even in complex and conflict-ridden child protection work, has found that: 'parents value professionals who give clear explanations, are open and honest and treat them with respect and dignity' (Cleaver and Walker, 2004:61).

In addition to this partnership with parents, the *Framework for the Assessment of Children in Need and their Families* requires social workers and other professionals involved in assessment work to involve children in the process of assessment.

Every assessment must be informed by the views of the child as well as the family. Children should, wherever possible, be seen alone and local authority children's social care has a duty to ascertain the child's wishes and feelings regarding the provision of services to be delivered (section 17 of the Children Act 1989, amended by section 53 Children Act 2004).

HM Government, 2013:21

The requirements for the participation of children and respect for their rights to be listened to and have their views heard in all matters concerning them as laid out in Article 12 UNCRC are discussed more fully along with other rights and entitlements in Chapter 3. Following an assessment and in the spirit of partnership working, parent(s) and child (if appropriate) should be informed in writing, and/or in another more appropriate medium, of the decisions made and be invited to record their views about and any disagreement with the information collated. This sharing of information should also extend to the agencies and individuals involved in the assessment.

The quality of assessment is also important and there is certainly a relationship between good outcomes and a good assessment and, similarly, for inadequate assessment and poor outcomes:

> ... there is evidence that the absence of assessments of maltreated children at different stages of professional involvement is related to repeat abuse ... and shortcomings in assessments have been a consistent feature in many cases of severe injury or child death ... Delays in assessment and decision-making in relation to the removal from home and placement of children can lead to difficulties in achieving permanent placements, and successful placements get harder with the child's increasing age; indeed, because of such delays some children never achieve a permanent placement ... Poor assessments may expose children to risks of further maltreatment or placement breakdown.
>
> *Turney et al., 2011:3*

It is thus crucial that social workers are familiar with the processes and theories which inform assessment practice. Holland (2011) examines the underpinning legislation and the range of theories which social workers draw on in assessment practice, as well as the designs and various approaches which are used to undertake assessment. Assessment work is complex and requires sustained attention to the advice and recommendations in the guidance. Social work students when first introduced to assessment during their training are surprised that there is no pro forma as such: instead of being a tick-box or checklist approach, assessment is an holistic in-depth examination.

1 How might you encourage the involvement of parents who are reluctant to engage in an assessment?
2 What sort of questions might parents and children have about the assessment process?

Common Assessment Framework

Where it is clear that the needs of a child can only be met by multiple agencies, the Common Assessment Framework (CAF) should be used. The CAF is based on the *Framework for Assessment* but also draws on other assessment approaches and is designed to promote a coordinated approach to assessment involving several agencies, including teachers, social workers, health visitors and professionals in community-based and voluntary sector organizations. These may be national organizations, such as Barnardo's or the Children's Society, or local providers. The CAF is offered to children who have additional needs to those being met by universal services. Unless a child is presenting a need, it is unlikely the CAF will be offered. The practitioner assesses needs using the CAF. The CAF is not a risk assessment. If a child or young person reveals they are at risk, the practitioner should follow the local safeguarding process immediately (DfE, 2012).

The CAF is a four-step process whereby practitioners identify a child's or young person's needs early, they assess those needs, deliver coordinated services and review progress. The CAF is designed to be used when:

- a practitioner is worried about how well a child or young person is progressing (e.g. concerns about their health, development, welfare, behaviour, progress in learning or any other aspect of their well-being);
- a child or young person, or their parent/carer, raises a concern with a practitioner;
- a child's or young person's needs are unclear, or broader than the practitioner's service can address.

The process is voluntary and informed consent is mandatory. Families do not have to engage but, if they do, they can choose what information they want to share. Children and families should not feel stigmatized by the CAF and they can request for a CAF to be initiated. The CAF process is not a 'referral' process but a 'request for services' (DfE, 2012). The CAF should identify what help the child and family require to prevent needs escalating to a point where they need a statutory assessment under the Children Act 1989 (HM Government, 2013).

The early help assessment should be undertaken by a lead professional who should provide support to the child and family, act as an advocate on their behalf and coordinate the delivery of support services. The lead professional role could be undertaken by a general practitioner, family support worker, teacher, health visitor and/or SEN coordinator. Decisions about who should be the lead professional should be taken on a case-by-case basis.

> *On-the-spot question*
>
> Think of an example of a case of a child you have worked with where a CAF would be appropriate. How did the CAF process prevent escalation of problems?

Core assessment

A core assessment is defined as an in-depth assessment which addresses the central or most important aspects of the needs of a child and the capacity of his or her parents or caregivers to respond appropriately to these needs within the wider family and community context. While this assessment is led by social services, it will invariably involve other agencies or independent professionals who will either provide information they hold about the child or parents, contribute specialist knowledge or advice to social services or undertake specialist assessments. Specific assessments of the child and/or family members may have already been undertaken prior to referral to the social services department. The findings from these should inform this assessment.

At the conclusion of this phase of assessment there should be an analysis of the findings which will provide an understanding of the child's circumstances and inform planning, case objectives and the nature of service provision. The timescale for completion of the core assessment is a maximum of 35 working days. A core assessment is deemed to have commenced at the point the initial assessment ended, or a strategy discussion decided to initiate enquiries under s. 47 Children Act 1989, or new information obtained on an open case indicates a core assessment should be undertaken. Where specialist assessments have been commissioned by social services from other agencies or independent professionals, it is recognized that they will not necessarily be completed within the 35-working-day period. Appropriate services should be provided whilst awaiting the completion of the specialist assessment.

Timescales

> The timeliness of an assessment is a critical element of the quality of that assessment and the outcomes for the child. The speed with which an assessment is carried out after a child's case has been referred into local authority children's social care should be determined by the needs of the individual child and the nature and level of any risk of harm faced by the child. This will require judgements to be made by the social worker in discussion with their manager on each individual case.
>
> *HM Government, 2013:23*

The *Framework for Assessment of Children in Need and their Families* stipulated the timescales which social workers undertaking assessment should adhere to (see DH, 2000:32). However, research has consistently suggested that the rigidity of compliance with these timescales was often at the expense of producing a good quality, thorough and appropriate assessment (see, for example, Broadhurst et al., 2009). Eileen Munro was tasked to undertake a review of child safeguarding (Munro, 2011) and, in her progress report (Munro, 2012), the emphasis on the timescales and their impact on assessment was raised again.

> Data such as timescales that began life as intelligent indirect measures of the quality of help children received became the direct goal of practice. The guidance also proliferated over the years with the original prescription of goals being increasingly augmented with prescription of how to achieve them, thereby creating increasing obstacles to flexibility and reform at the local level.
>
> *Munro, 2012:9*

In terms of the removal of the fixed assessment timescales, Munro (2012) argues that the experience of the trial authorities, which are exempt from imposing statutory timescales, has been positive. In particular, the relaxation of these timescales has led to improvement in assessment, including prioritizing work and reflective practice.

In regards to a referral for assessment, *Working Together* stipulates:

> Within one working day of a referral being received, a local authority social worker should make a decision about the type of response that is required and acknowledge receipt to the referrer. (DfE, 2013c:23)

If immediate action is needed to protect a child this must be provided as soon after the referral as possible. Where an assessment is undertaken:

> The maximum timeframe for the assessment to conclude, such that it is possible to reach a decision on next steps, should be no longer than 45 working days from the point of referral. If, in discussion with a child and their family and other professionals, an assessment exceeds 45 working days the social worker should record the reasons for exceeding the time limit.
>
> *DfE, 2013c:23*

The social worker should also explain to the child and their family how the assessment will be carried out and when they can expect a decision on next steps.

PRACTICE FOCUS

In the case of *R (on the Application of SJ and Another) v Surrey County Council* [2014] discussed above (see page 35), the timescales were lengthy and the needs of the children involved changed over time.

- Why do you think timescales for completion of assessments are important for children, parents and social workers?
- What do you think are the challenges to undertaking assessment work within these defined timescales?

The role of the third sector in providing services to children in need of support

The third sector, which includes voluntary and not-for-profit, charity and community sector organizations and social enterprise schemes, is becoming increasingly attractive to local authorities who must provide cost-effectiveness and greater flexibility in their s. 17 Children Act 1989 services to children in need and their families. Third-sector organizations are able to offer local and accessible services; they can draw on funding from a range of sources and give greater choice and responsiveness to service users. In recent years, government investment in these types of services has been significantly cut, however, community-based and managed provision are a valuable resource for local authorities and social workers are encouraged to engage with these community-based family support services which children in need and their families are more likely to engage with when they are in difficulties.

Children England is a membership organization for large and small voluntary sector organizations in England working with children, young people and families. In its report to the Office of the Third Sector, Children England highlights how the models of work in the sector differ from statutory provision:

> ... there is support for seeing children and families as individuals with capacities and aspirations, rather than traditional statutory models where they are seen as having 'problems', 'conditions' and 'gaps.' This should come as no surprise as the voluntary and community sector has built itself on a long history of empowering children and families, taking a flexible needs-based approach in supporting them and building long-term relationships with the people who use services ...
>
> *Children England, 2010:2*

Children England advocates partnership models of working with children and families and so it is involved in the design and development of services to ensure they are tailored to meet needs. This is specifically discussed in relation to the 'personalization agenda' which affects children with disabilities and their families. The personalization agenda has seen a shift from providing a one-size-fits-all service to children with disabilities and their families to a much more bespoke service which can adapt and respond to changes in circumstances and needs (Children England, 2010).

On-the-spot question

What statutory and community/voluntary sector services are available in your local authority area to support children who are assessed as in need?

Community-based models of support to children in need

Community-based organizations have always provided some assistance for children and their families, indeed the voluntary and informal UK sector includes some of the biggest child welfare charities, such as Barnardo's, NCH Action for Children, Rathbones, Homestart etc. Research on models of practice suggests a community-based models approach empowers children and families to make decisions and take action together. Working with children in need and their families in this way promotes a sense of achievement for families under pressure and can lead to reduced likelihood of statutory intervention. As in all family support provisions, time, resources and careful planning are needed, as well as review mechanisms.

Sure Start and children's centres were a central plank of New Labour's child care policy during its term in office. The premise underpinning these schemes was to provide accessible, local support for families in areas where there were high levels of deprivation. As well as providing affordable child care, Sure Start and children's centres developed a range of services in partnership with local communities, and became the first point of call for children and their families who needed various levels of support. The funding of such schemes has reduced since the initial roll-out, however, local authorities continue to draw resources together to sustain these schemes, recognizing that the early work they carry out often prevents families from needing to be referred to statutory and safe-guarding services. The section below, from the Office for Standards in Education (OFSTED) (2011), illustrates the range of work being undertaken in one Sure Start centre in Blackpool which has been highlighted as good practice.

Sure Start and children's centres

Sure Start programmes were introduced to bring integrated child welfare and support services at the community level, recognizing that some families access help at an early stage. Sure Start is able to put families in contact with several agencies. Talbot and Brunswick Sure Start is one such scheme and was designated as a phase one children's centre in 2005. The OFSTED (2011) report on this centre, located in the town centre ward of Talbot and Brunswick in Blackpool, provides a good example of the potential of this community-based early intervention model.

A traditional seaside resort, Blackpool is economically and socially disadvantaged, being ranked in the top 30 per cent of the most deprived areas in the country. A large majority of children attending the nursery live in the 10 per cent most deprived areas. A high proportion of families are from White British heritage backgrounds and a small percentage from a wide range of other ethnic heritages. Blackpool is well known for its transient population. Many families in the area have only seasonal employment and move in and out of the town between jobs. Many families live in the area only for a short period before they move to accommodation in other parts of the town. Average income levels are amongst the lowest nationally and 37.7 per cent of children aged nought to four live in households where no one is working.

The centre shares its building with health services and is part of a campus, which includes a community development base, children's park, public garden and large play barn. The centre delivers outreach services from other local premises, including schools, churches, general practitioner surgeries and a leisure centre. An advisory board oversees the work of the centre and is accountable to the local authority. Through the local authority the centre is the registered body for the on-site nursery. Most children enter early education with a much lower range of skills than that expected for their age.

The centre has been developed with local people as well as an exemplary range of partners and a highly skilled staff team. The provision is outstanding and it is strongly integrated, cohesive and innovative. As a result, children and families make outstanding progress in most outcomes, whilst also facing the most challenging of circumstances. The depth of commitment by all staff and partners to improving outcomes and tackling poverty is a key strength. Many people move in and out of the area but the centre makes rapid and tailored assessments of family needs.

Leadership and management of the centre are outstanding. Working quietly and passionately, the centre manager makes highly effective use of parents' views and expertise, the staff team and of resources. As a result, the centre is giving outstanding value for money. All leaders, staff and partners have a clear and sophisticated understanding of the strengths and priorities of the centre and this leads to continuous improvement. This is complemented by an excellent knowledge of the local community. The centre pursues inclusion for all children and families and treats people with respect and dignity. As a consequence, the centre's commitment to equality of opportunity and diversity is strong (OFSTED, 2011).

Family group conferencing

A family group conference is a meeting about a child in a family which is led by family members who plan and make decisions for the child. Children and young people are normally involved in their own family group conference, although often with support from an advocate. Family group conferencing (FGC) is voluntary and families cannot be forced to have a family group conference (Family Rights Group, 2013). Family group conferences can be used in any serious situation where a plan and decision needs to be made about a vulnerable child.

FGC draws upon Maori culture and its development was a response to the large number of Maori children being removed into state institutions. FGC is now recognized in law (Children, Young Persons and their Families Act 1989) in New Zealand as being the key process by which families make informed and responsible decisions, recommendations and plans for their children and young people. FGC can be used whenever a situation is sufficiently serious that a plan and decisions need to be made about a vulnerable child or adult. They are now being used in the UK in all areas of child welfare including in:

- preventative services;
- safeguarding work;
- court proceedings, both private and public law;
- looked after children and planning for leaving care;
- education (truancy and exclusions);
- anti-social behaviour and youth justice, including restorative justice;
- domestic violence (Family Rights Group, 2013).

Three-quarters of local authorities in England and Wales currently run or commission FGC for children in their area or are planning to do so. However, at present only a small number of councils routinely offer families FGC before a young child is taken into care. In the UK FGC is used particularly when a child is at risk of going into care, although some local areas are using the approach to prevent school exclusions, tackle anti-social behaviour, or to address youth offending (Family Rights Group, 2013).

Families, including extended family members, are assisted by an FGC coordinator to prepare for the meeting. At the start of the meeting, social workers and other professionals set out their concerns about the child and outline what support is available. The uniqueness of this approach is that, in the second part of the meeting, the family discusses and agrees on a plan for the child, taking ownership and control of the meeting and defining its own responses. The family is then supported to carry out the plan. This would be an approach which would fit in well with assessment of children in need where there are some concerns about their welfare but also some identified strengths in the family and extended family which could be drawn on to support the child.

Practitioners need to exercise caution in using FGC to work with families where there has been domestic violence. Indeed, any intervention which seeks to work with families to develop their own responses needs to account for the power distribution in families with a history of abuse. FGC is not a cheap alternative and requires resources as well as advocacy, review and support. The interventions decided upon by the family also need to be available otherwise the plan will not work.

> *On-the-spot question*
>
> Why do you think families with a child in need of support might resist or welcome this type of support?

PRACTICE FOCUS

In *R (on the Application of G) v Southwark London Borough Council* [2009] the family situation broke down and mediation was attempted but also broke down (see pages 26–27). To what extent might G have benefited from FGC? List the issues that might have been addressed in taking this approach.

• How would you present this approach to G and his family?

Pyramid clubs

Developed in the 1970s in the UK, pyramid clubs offer a therapeutic group-work early intervention for children aged 7–14. The clubs run for ten weeks for 1.5 hours a week, offering a developmental journey for those children who internalize their difficulties and are showing early signs of mental health problems, such as social withdrawal, somatic disorders, depression and anxiety. Pyramid clubs were developed drawing on cognitive psychology and positive psychology. They deliver an experiential model which helps children and young people to learn to manage their thoughts and feelings in a supportive environment. Over 33,000 children and young people have attended pyramid clubs across England, Wales and Northern Ireland.

The pyramid approach is centred upon a philosophy of early intervention: '… working with children at the early signs of problems developing, rather than waiting for full-blown mental health difficulties to develop' (ContinYou, 2013).

Pyramid therapeutic activity clubs are designed for children who are quiet, shy, anxious, isolated, withdrawn or finding it difficult to make friends. They aim to provide children with a fun, positive experience, in a group, with new experiences and chances to develop friendships. Pyramid clubs are designed for children of all sorts of ability and background and use a systematic approach to ensure that the children who need support are identified early so that the support given is low-key and non-stigmatizing. The outcomes for the child have been identified as:

- a sense of belonging;
- increased self-esteem and confidence;
- ability to make new friendships;
- improved academic performance;
- more willing to participate;
- better relationships with peers and adults;
- improvement in self-concept/locus of control;
- better social skills;
- improved attendance and attitude towards school.

Pyramid also offers a complementary or standalone model of support for parents/carers. These groups are specially designed to enhance the skills of parents to promote their child's emotional well-being. The groups provide an opportunity for parents to get together and share experiences, supporting each other to enhance their relationships with their children. There is evidence that parents are finding the course a confidence-building stepping-stone that helps them move on to other more targeted parent support programmes, or to family learning or work (Children England, 2010).

The difficulties in access to services which local authorities have a duty to provide are compounded by gatekeeping and a reduction in services as well as a tendency to assess but then not provide a service. Assessment is crucial to determining access to limited resources. This chapter discussed the importance of working in partnership with parents as part of the assessment process, again another central principle of the Children Act 1989. There is a wide range of professionals based in both statutory and non-statutory and third-sector organizations who undertake assessment work with children in need of support and their families. Parents and the children in many cases and with appropriate support and assistance are able to find answers and resources with advice from professionals. The models of community-based services often draw on local established networks and promote their participation and involvement.

Further reading

Holland, S (2011) *Child and Family Assessment in Social Work Practice.* This book draws on research evidence to support different approaches to assessment and, in particular, discusses the balance needed in assessment work to ensure that children and young people and their parents are active participants in the process.

Family Rights Group www.frg.org.uk is an organization that works across England and Wales. It promotes policies and practices that help children to be raised safely and securely within their families. It also campaigns for support to assist family, friends and carers, including grandparents who are raising children who cannot live at home, and provides advice sheets on its website for parents and carers who are involved in children's services.

Turney, D, D Platt, J Selwyn and E Farmer (2011) *Social Work Assessment of Children in Need: What Do We Know? Messages from Research.* This publication discusses studies of assessment and outcomes in social work over a ten-year period and provides the reader with detailed information on assessment practice. The findings of the study reinforce the view that evidence-based knowledge and theory support good assessment practice.

3

CHILDREN IN NEED AND CHILDREN'S RIGHTS

AT A GLANCE THIS CHAPTER COVERS:

- best interests of the child principle
- the UNCRC framework and the needs of children
- children's rights perspective in domestic legislation and statutory guidance
- competence and children's rights to participate as citizens
- the UK record on promoting the rights of children

The UNCRC and the European Convention on Human Rights 1950 (ECHR) determine to a great extent how local authorities and the government define and respond to children in the UK. However, the extent to which the Conventions and their Articles inform practice with children in need requires some discussion. Children without parental care, including children who may be living in institutional care or in foster care, are often supported by organizations which campaign for improvements to children's rights in terms of the services they receive and are entitled to (see, for example, National Youth Advocacy Service (NYAS)). Local authorities are duty bound to provide or commission children's rights services for looked after children. Similarly, children in need have entitlements to rights and this chapter discusses the requirements and duties related to the exercise of children's rights and the tensions in promoting children's rights perspectives for children in need and their families.

The HRA and the ECHR

The UK has been a party to the ECHR since 1951 and domesticated the ECHR in 1998 with the introduction of the HRA. This essentially made the ECHR enforceable in UK law and ensured compliance between the ECHR and domestic legislation. There are three rights contained in the ECHR in regard to children in need and their families which are highly relevant:

- **Article 3:** the prohibition against torture and inhuman or degrading treatment;
- **Article 8:** the right to respect for private and family life;
- **Article 14:** the prohibition of discrimination.

Article 8 ECHR has been utilized by the European Court. In *Saviny v Ukraine* (2010) the decision for the children of parents who were blind to go into care was disputed as there had been a lack of evidence and consideration of less drastic action to promote and improve the welfare of the children.

In this case the parents appealed on the basis that no danger to the children had been established, and that it was impossible for them to provide better conditions for the children because of their blindness. Their appeal was dismissed. The parents also claimed that the decision to take the children into care had breached their right to respect for family life under Article 8 ECHR. If a decision to remove a child from the family home was explained in terms of the need to protect the child from danger, the existence of such a danger should be actually established; the mere fact that a child could be placed in a more beneficial environment does not on its own justify compulsory removal. Nor could the parents' precarious situation justify removal, as this could be addressed by less radical means, such as targeted financial assistance and social counselling. Although relevant, the authorities' reasons for removing the children were not sufficient; there had been insufficient evidence to support the claims of the authorities; there had been no in-depth analysis of the extent to which the reported inadequacies related to the parents' personal qualities, or to financial difficulties and objective frustrations, which could have been addressed; and at no stage had the children's own views been sought, including the eldest, aged 13 at the time. There had been a violation of Article 8 ECHR.

In making this decision the court considered that the severance of family ties meant cutting a child off from its roots, which could only be justified in exceptional circumstances. Therefore, a relevant decision had to be supported by sufficiently sound and weighty considerations in the interests of the child, and it was for the respondent state to establish that a careful assessment of the impact of the proposed care measure on the parents and the child had been made. This suggests that social work assessments should take into account that removal should only go ahead with clear evidence that children are at risk of significant harm. To do otherwise is to infringe the rights of the children and parents to their family life.

Furthermore, at no stage of the proceedings had the children been heard by the judges and, not only had the children been separated from their family of origin, they had also been placed in different institutions. Two of them had lived in another city, which had rendered it difficult to maintain regular contact. Accordingly, although the reasons given by the national authorities for removal of the applicants' children had been relevant, they had not been sufficient to have justified such a serious interference with the applicants' family life.

The right to private and family life has received broad interpretation by the European Court of Human Rights and in the UK. Private life includes personal autonomy, physical and psychological integrity and aspects of social and physical identity. Unjustified interference with this right essentially forbids the state from taking steps which are in conflict with protecting the integrity of privacy in family life. In some circumstances this might

> **KEY CASE ANALYSIS**

R (MXL and Others) v Secretary of State for the Home Department [2010]

The state is also required to uphold the best interests of children as can be seen in this case. A Jamaican woman was detained using immigration powers which resulted in being separated from her children. The High Court held that the UK Border Agency (UKBA) had not given primary consideration to the best interests of two children when deciding to detain and continue the detention of their mother and criticized immigration judges who refused to grant immigration bail to the mother, and thus failed to give primary consideration to the children's best interests. The High Court found the mother's detention to have been unlawful. The judge referred to the interests of the child as being a primary consideration which should be applied by public officials (including immigration judges) when making immigration decisions that have an impact on the welfare of children. Moreover, these decisions are not merely decisions about domestic law but fall within the realms of international legislation and specifically the ECHR.

This draws attention to the issue that the detention was prolonged and consideration of the impact of this on MXL's children was not taken into account.

When the interests of children are affected, this means that other principles of international law binding on contracting states should be complied with. In the case of children, those principles are reflected in Article 3(1) UNCRC: 'Article 3(1): the best interests of the child as a primary consideration in all actions concerning children.'

According to Mr Justice Blake:

> The principle requires active measures throughout Government, parliament and the judiciary. Every legislative, administrative and judicial body or institution is required to apply the best interests principle by systematically considering how children's rights and interests are or will be affected by their decisions and actions – by, for example, a proposed or existing law or policy or administrative action or court decision, including those which are not directly concerned with children, but indirectly affect children. [83]

mean providing welfare support to enable family life. as in *Anufrijeva v London Borough of Southwark* [2003]. This was a case involving immigration **detention** and the Administrative Court of the Queen's Bench Division held that the claimant's continued detention after an order for reconsideration of an appeal against her deportation was unlawful, as the assessments failed to take into account the welfare of her two children, with the result that the decision was in violation of Articles 5 (the right to liberty and security) and 8 (the right to family life) ECHR, and therefore contrary to domestic law.

The UNCRC

The origins of the UNCRC lie in the Children's Charter of 1923 proposed by Eglantyne Jebb who founded the Save the Children Fund. The perception of children having rights and entitlements has advanced dramatically since then and the UNCRC is now almost a quarter of a century old. The rights of children to be protected from harm, abuse and exploitation are well embedded in UK policy terms. The participation of children, however, has been less progressive and much more controversial:

> Children's limitations, in terms of physical dependency, emotional and intellectual immaturity, have all been advanced as apparently irrefutable arguments for postponing their assumption of adult rights and responsibilities. (Jenkins, 1995:35)

This is especially pertinent in regard to children who are the subject of state intervention through social work.

The UNCRC is an international human rights treaty that grants all children and young people a comprehensive set of rights. The UK signed the UNCRC on 19 April 1990, ratified it on 16 December 1991 and it came into force on 15 January 1992. The UNCRC applies to children who are defined as being from birth to 18 years old. The UNCRC is the most widely ratified international human rights treaty and the only international human rights treaty to include civil, political, economic, social and cultural rights. It sets out in detail what every child needs to have a safe, happy and fulfilled childhood regardless of their sex, religion, social origin, and where and to whom they were born. This Convention is also the only international human rights treaty that expressly gives non-governmental organizations (NGOs) a role in monitoring its implementation (Children's Rights International Network (CRIN), 2013).

The UNCRC gives children and young people more than 40 substantive rights, including the right to:

- special protection measures and assistance;
- access to services such as education and healthcare;
- develop their personalities, abilities and talents to the fullest potential;
- grow up in an environment of happiness, love and understanding;
- be informed about and participate in achieving their rights in an accessible and active manner.

The UNCRC is not legislation and should not be confused with such. The UNCRC provides a broad international framework to inform domestic legislation. A link to the full text of the UNCRC can be found at the end of this chapter. UK legislation is measured for compliance with this and with other international treaties.

UNCRC Articles relevant to children in need of support

Article 3 UNCRC as discussed above refers to the best interests of children. This must be the primary concern in making decisions that may affect them and adults should do what is best for children when they make decisions and they should think about how these decisions will affect children. This also applies to budget, policy and law-makers and the state must do its utmost to implement these rights. Article 5 UNCRC requires states to respect the responsibilities, rights and duties of parents, or extended family, or community, or legal guardians, or other persons legally responsible for the child, to provide, in a manner consistent with the evolving capacities of the child, appropriate direction and guidance. This is particularly important in contexts where children and families are being assessed and is a recognition that with support families can often find resolutions to their issues and concerns and this right should be respected by those who are working with families. Article 6 UNCRC is concerned with the right to life and survival and development. Children have the right to live and governments should ensure that children survive and develop healthily. Article 9 UNCRC refers to children being separated from their parents:

Article 9

> except when competent authorities subject to judicial review
> determine, in accordance with applicable law and procedures, that
> such separation is necessary for the best interests of the child. Such

determination may be necessary in a particular case such as one involving abuse or neglect of the child by the parents, or one where the parents are living separately and a decision must be made as to the child's place of residence.

UNCRC

As discussed in Chapter 2, a thorough, transparent and detailed assessment process would ensure that any decisions to remove a child were in the child's best interests. The assessment process would also in effect document why being with the parents was in the child's best interests.

An important Article in the context of this discussion about children in need is Article 12 UNCRC which is concerned with respect for the views of the child:

When adults are making decisions that affect children, children have the right to say what they think should happen and have their opinions taken into account. This does not mean that children can now tell their parents what to do. This Convention encourages adults to listen to the opinions of children and involve them in decision-making – not give children authority over adults. Article 12 UNCRC does not interfere with parents' right and responsibility to express their views on matters affecting their children. Moreover, the Convention recognises that the level of a child's participation in decisions must be appropriate to the child's level of maturity. Children's ability to form and express their opinions develops with age and most adults will naturally give the views of teenagers greater weight than those of a pre-schooler, whether in family, legal or administrative decisions.

CRIN, 2013

Article 12 UNCRC directly relates to assessment practice (as discussed in Chapter 2) whereby due consideration is given to the voices of children being assessed and children are consulted about decisions about services and interventions decided upon. Children should also be asked to evaluate the services they receive.

Article 13 UNCRC is concerned with freedom of expression, and Article 14 UNCRC with freedom of thought, conscience and religion and both are relevant in terms of ensuring that, when children in need of support are being assessed, their cultural and religious/faith beliefs are respected in the process and in determining any intervention to meet the assessed needs. Article 18 UNCRC is concerned with parental responsibility as in

s. 2 Children Act 1989. Whilst Article 19 UNCRC deals with the protection from abuse and neglect by parents, it also refers to protective measures which should see the establishment of social programmes to provide support for the child and for those who have the care of the child. In addition, provision should be made of other forms of prevention and identification, reporting, referral, investigation, treatment and review processes. Again this relates to the duty under s. 17 Children Act 1989 to identify children in need, and provide services to support families.

Article 20 UNCRC concerns children with a family and their protection and Article 22 with refugee children (discussed further in Chapter 4). Article 23 UNCRC deals with the rights of children with disabilities (discussed in more detail in Chapter 5):

Article 23

> A disabled child has the right to special care, education and training to help him or her enjoy a full and decent life in dignity and achieve the greatest degree of self-reliance and social integration possible.
>
> *UNCRC*

Article 24 UNCRC outlines the health rights of children, which are directly relevant to children in need of support:

Article 24

> States Parties recognize the right of the child to the enjoyment of the highest attainable standard of health and to facilities for the treatment of illness and rehabilitation of health. States Parties shall strive to ensure that no child is deprived of his or her right of access to such health care services.
>
> *UNCRC*

Article 25 UNCRC provides for the rights of children in care to have the placement reviewed.

Articles 26 and 27 UNCRC are concerned with the rights of children to have a standard of living adequate for their physical, mental, spiritual, moral and social development and so is also relevant to this discussion in relation to the local authorities' s. 17 Children Act 1989 duty to provide services to children in need in their area. Articles 28 and 29 UNCRC are both about rights to education and Article 31 UNCRC confers on children the right to play, leisure and cultural activities. The entitlement of children to protection from abuse or exploitation is contained in Article 34 UNCRC. For the purpose of this discussion of children in need of support, Articles

37, 39 and 40 UNCRC are relevant to those children who have been found to have harmful sexual behaviour (discussed further in Chapter 7) and their rights to treatment which recognizes their dignity and worth.

On-the-spot question

To what extent can social workers who are working with children in need of support ensure that they are enhancing or protecting the rights of children in their work?

Children's rights in UK domestic legislation

Listening to children's wishes and feelings and the participation of children in decisions about them are two key rights which children in need of support are entitled to. The duty to consult with children was introduced by the Children Act 1989, in relation to both court proceedings for all children and local authority decision-making for looked after children. The Children Act 2004 amended the Children Act 1989 to include the requirement that the wishes and feelings of children in need under s. 17 were included and given due consideration in matters relating to them. Like a court, local authorities have a duty to listen and take account of children, although the caveat 'as far is as reasonably practicable', which may be about the availability of resources, might affect the availability of these services in local authorities.

Working Together to Safeguard Children (HM Government, 2013) states that interventions need to be child-centred and this is what children have said that they need:

- vigilance: to have adults notice when things are troubling them;
- understanding and action: to understand what is happening, to be heard and understood and to have that understanding acted upon;
- stability: to be able to develop an ongoing stable relationship of trust with those helping them;
- respect: to be treated with the expectation that they are competent rather than not;
- information and engagement: to be informed about and involved in procedures, decisions, concerns and plans;
- explanation: to be informed of the outcome of assessments and decisions and reasons when their views have not met with a positive response;

- support: to be provided with support in their own right as well as a member of their family;
- advocacy: to be provided with advocacy to assist them in putting forward their views.

The Children's Commissioner

Part 1 of the Children Act 2004 established the office of Children's Commissioner and in doing so reiterated a commitment to promoting children's rights perspectives in legislation and policy related to children and young people. The role of the Children's Commissioner is to promote the views of children and young people from birth to 18 (up to 21 for young people in care or with learning difficulties).

The Children's Commissioner has the function of promoting awareness of the views and interests of children in England. The Children's Commissioner may:

s. 2(1)

    (a) encourage persons exercising functions or engaged in activities affecting children to take account of their views and interests;
    (b) advise the Secretary of State on the views and interests of children;
    (c) consider or research the operation of complaints procedures so far as relating to children;
    (d) consider or research any other matter relating to the interests of children;
    (e) publish a report on any matter considered or researched by him under this section.
(3) The Children's Commissioner is to be concerned in particular under this section with the views and interests of children so far as relating to the following aspects of their well-being:
    (a) physical and mental health and emotional well-being;
    (b) protection from harm and neglect;
    (c) education, training and recreation;
    (d) the contribution made by them to society;
    (e) social and economic well-being.

Children Act 2004

In a report about the Children's Commissioner in England (DfE, 2010), the impact of the office of the Commissioner was described as disappointing, principally because of the limited remit:

> The issue of children's rights is emotive and complex. Nonetheless, there is a striking degree of unanimity in the evidence presented to me that the statutory basis of the Children's Commissioner should refer to children's rights, in place of their views and interests. There is also a strong implication in much of the evidence that the lack of a clear focus in the work of the OCC over the last six years has in part been due to the lack of clarity in the legislation.
>
> *DfE, 2010:22*

The combined efforts of the Children's Commissioners in the UK can promote the rights of children and pose solid questions to the government about the minimization of these rights. In 2011, the four Children's Commissioners, in their interim report to the UNCRC, identified that spending cuts and high levels of persistent poverty were impacting on children (Children's Commissioner, 2011). The changes implemented by the Welfare Reform Act 2012 include: a reduction in support for childcare; the introduction of Universal Credit; a potential cap on benefit levels; and the introduction of conditionality in benefit payments. It is argued by anti-poverty campaigners that these measures have driven vulnerable children, young people and their families into poverty and pushed them toward needing support from specialist and not universal services. Larkins et al. (2012) illustrate the impact of these welfare reforms in a study which was co-produced using participatory research with children and young people.

Advocacy

In England, potentially all looked after children, care leavers and those assessed as 'in need' have a legal right to advocacy support when they want to make a complaint or representation. Statutory guidance has extended the scope of advocacy to 'looked after children' in the care planning and review process and to care leavers, particularly when moving from their care placement. However, there has been no corresponding development for 'children in need' other than already provided for in *Working Together* (HM Government, 2013) in relation to support at child protection conferences.

The Mental Capacity Act 2005 established the role of the Independent Mental Capacity Advocate (IMCA). The IMCA service came into effect in England in April 2007. The IMCA service is provided for any person aged

16 years or older who has nobody who is able to support and represent them, other than paid staff, and who lacks capacity to make a decision about specified issues. If a person who lacks capacity already has an advocate, they may still be entitled to an IMCA, but the IMCA would consult with their advocate. Local authorities in England commission IMCA services. Section 130A Mental Health Act 1983, inserted by the Mental Health Act 2007, states that all children and young people, irrespective of age, who have been sectioned under the Mental Health Act 1983, or who are likely to be sectioned, have the right to an Independent Mental Health Advocate. They also have the right to an advocate, as voluntary patients, if their clinician is considering giving them electro-convulsive therapy. The Mental Health Act 1983 states that advocates must be allowed to talk to children and young people in private, they must also be allowed to talk to the clinician and read any relevant medical records.

Statutory entitlements that are included in legislation for looked after children, care leavers and children in need in making complaints and representations, and for young people aged 16 and over for representation if they are judged to lack capacity, and for those sectioned or in other circumstances under mental health legislation include:

- statutory guidance: for looked after children in care planning and reviews and for care leavers;
- national minimum standards: for looked after children in foster and residential care;
- provision of accommodation for 16 and 17-year-old young people who may be homeless and/or require accommodation;
- under the rules for secure training centres: for young people detained in a secure training centre to have access to an independent person.

In regard to the last point regarding the role of the independent person:

> Although the term 'independent person' is used in the rules, in practice the function of an independent person in this context is that of an advocate. This has been adopted by the Youth Justice Board in its contractual arrangements with independent agencies who are commissioned to provide advocacy to young people in Young Offender Institutions (YOIs) and Secure Training Centres (STCs). This gives the young person the right to access support and representation from an independent advocate whilst in the secure estate.
>
> *Children's Commissioner, 2011:20*

The Children Act 1989 Act gave the right to looked after children, and children in need, to make representations and complaints. This was extended to care leavers in the Children (Leaving Care) Act 2000. The legal right giving support to children to exercise these rights was included in s. 119 Adoption and Children Act 2002. Local authorities are now under a duty to make arrangements to assist looked after children, care leavers and children in need who want to make a complaint. The amendment to the legislation was accompanied by the *Get it Sorted* regulations and guidance (DfES, 2004).

On-the-spot question	Why is it important that a child in need should have access to an advocate to support them when making a complaint about a service they have received or about an individual?

Children's rights organizations have tended to focus on providing advocacy for children who are looked after and those in the criminal justice system to have their views listened to and to participate in meetings and decision-making processes. However, there are strong arguments in favour of also promoting the rights of children who are in need to access advocacy services. It is of course crucial that children who are being looked after by local authorities have regular supported access to children's rights officers and organizations which ensure the voices of these children and young people are listened to by policy-makers and practitioners. Given that there are a great many more children and young people in need of support it is clear that they should also be aware of their rights and how to access them. However, this position is controversial not least because of the resourcing and promoting of and enabling access to advocacy and children rights. Quite simply put, ensuring that children have their rights is a costly and resource-intensive business.

Children, young people and competence

Research has found that children are capable of responding to difficult and challenging questions about themselves and their future. Children's competence to make decisions is not only dependent upon their qualities, but also the situation they are in and the support available to them (Thomas, 2002). Children do not suddenly become competent to advocate for their own interests and make decisions for

> **PRACTICE FOCUS**
>
> Daniel is aged 15 and has physical and learning disabilities and receives support as he is a child in need. Daniel is listed on the register of disabled children in his local authority. He lives with his mother (his main carer), but has had no contact with his father since his parents separated when he was seven. His parents were never married. Daniel is accommodated under s. 20 Children Act 1989 and stays with a link family once a month. He also has respite care in a residential centre every week for one night. Daniel has never attended or participated in his six-monthly looked after child (LAC) review, his mother says he is not able to contribute due to his disabilities and usually speaks for him. At the review it is suggested by the independent reviewing officer that the social worker should contact Daniels's father to discuss him seeing Daniel and playing a greater role in his life.
>
> - What potential legal issues are there in this scenario?
> - How might the social worker ensure that Daniel's wishes and feelings are heard about the decision regarding the proposed contact with his father?
>
> Before the next review Daniel's mother dies very suddenly and decisions need to be made about Daniel's future care and welfare, including whom he should live with and who should provide care for him.
>
> - What legal issues need to be considered at Daniel's next LAC review?
> - What choices are there for the continued care and welfare of Daniel now that his mother is dead?

themselves, rather they develop this capacity through experience and opportunity (see Johns, 2014, in this series for further discussions of the development of competence). Factors affecting a child or young person's competence include: maturity and cognition; support and preparation; and the structure of the situation. Political and sexual rights are useful test cases for many arguments about what rights children should have and at what age. The right to vote is an index of participation in the wider community, with the implication that one's choices will have effects for other people. The right to take part in sexual activity and to make sexual relationships is an index of how far one is trusted to take charge of one's own body and well-being, and of one's moral life (Thomas, 2002).

There are key principles which should guide practitioners to elicit the views of children and young people which include explaining the context of the decision and what will happen to the information they provide. It is important to set aside time and use a range of verbal and non-verbal strategies to engage the child or young person in discussion about questions that they are considering, as well as providing clarity about the weight and responsibility of the child's views. It may take more than one meeting for children to grasp what is required of them and they may also need a written summary of what has been discussed and/or decided (Welbourne, 2012).

On-the-spot question	1 What approaches to eliciting and incorporating the views of children in assessment practice have you used?
	2 What difference has this made to your assessment or intervention?

Competence is best understood as a continuum and it is thus important to provide opportunities for children to develop their competence – this includes responding to them and then giving feedback when they have been invited to participate in decision-making either about themselves or about their circumstances (see Johns, 2014).

Monitoring children's rights in the UK

The realization of children's rights and the UK record on instituting these is monitored periodically by the UN Committee on the Rights of the Child. According to the report in 2008, the UK was not doing enough to protect children's privacy or to uphold the 'best interests of the child' when new policy and law was developed and the Committee expressed regret that the principle of the best interests of the child was not reflected as a primary consideration in all legislative and policy matters affecting children. The Committee did acknowledge that there was substantial legislation to strengthen and protect children's rights and important developments which include: the creation of the Children's Commissioners; the creation of the Equality and Human Rights Commission (EHRC); and the appointment of a Cabinet Minister for Children. In addition, the Committee was highly critical about the treatment of children in the criminal justice system, in care, education and in immigration, and responded by making a number of recommendations in these areas. Some of the key observations made by the Committee, and raised by the EHRC, included:

- Discrimination and social stigmatization continues to be experienced by certain groups of children: Roma and Irish travellers' children; migrant, asylum-seeking and refugee children; lesbian, bisexual, gay, and transgender children; and children belonging to minority groups.
- The Committee recommended raising the minimum age of criminal responsibility, which is the lowest in Europe (10 years).
- Regarding SEN and looked after children, the Committee found that the right to complain regarding educational provisions is restricted to parents, which presents problems especially for looked after children for whom local authorities have, though mostly do not use, parental authority. The Committee recommends that children without parental care have a representative who actively defends their best interests and that children who are able to express their views have an independent right to appeal to the SEN tribunals.
- Permanent and temporary school exclusions are still high and affect children from groups which in general are low on school achievement. The Committee recommends the use of the disciplinary measure of permanent or temporary exclusion as a means of last resort only; it also recommends a reduction in the number of exclusions and that social workers and educational psychologists be brought into school in order to help children in conflict with school.
- Asylum-seeking children continue to be detained, including those undergoing an age assessment who may be kept in detention for weeks until the assessment is completed. Data is inadequate and there is no independent oversight of reception conditions for unaccompanied children who have to be returned. Key recommendations include: intensifying efforts to ensure that detention of asylum-seeking and migrant children is always used as a measure of last resort and for the shortest appropriate period of time; the appointment of guardians to unaccompanied asylum-seekers and migrant children; ensuring that returns of unaccompanied asylum-seeker children happen with adequate safeguards, including an independent assessment of the conditions upon return, including family environment (Refugee Council, 2012a).

The next report of the UN Committee is due in 2014. There has clearly been some progress and achievements in the UK in relation to the observations and recommendations made in 2008, and yet there are several issues discussed in the chapters which follow which remain unaddressed, most notably the continued use of detention for separated and unaccompanied children and the low age of criminal responsibility which criminalizes children as young as 10 who have demonstrated harmful sexual behaviour.

The UNCRC is the international treaty which provides the broad framework for our domestic legislation in relation to children's rights. The involvement and participation of children is an important right for children enshrined in Article 12 UNCRC and particularly for the groups of children in need of support which the remaining chapters of this book discuss. Social workers undertaking assessment work with children in need of support are duty bound to uphold the rights of these children and promote their best interests in compliance not only with the domestic legislation but also with regard to the ECHR, HRA and UNCRC. This chapter also outlined the observations of the UN Committee on the Rights of the Child which expressed concerns about several issues related to children's rights, and of direct relevance to the groups of children in need of support who are discussed in this book.

Further reading

Children's Commissioners – there are four UK Children's Commissioners: England www.childrenscommissioner.gov.uk/info/about_us; Northern Ireland www.niccy.org; Wales www.childcom.org.uk/en/about-us; Scotland www.sccyp.org.uk.

CRIN's website www.crin.org/about/index.asp contains a wealth of valuable information, reports and factsheets related to children's rights globally. In addition to campaigning for children's rights, CRIN also monitors states' compliance with the UNCRC.

Dalrymple, J and J Hough (eds) (1995) *Having a Voice: An Exploration of Children's Rights and Advocacy* is an early edited collection of essays about the role of advocacy and is a useful resource for social workers who are reflecting on how to balance their roles as agents of the state with their duties to promote the welfare of children in need of support and ensure their active and meaningful participation.

Thomas, N (2002) *Children, Family and the State* (Bristol: Policy Press), 'Rights of childhood' (ch. 4), examines the theoretical and philosophical questions related to the rights of children to participate in decisions about their lives.

UNCRC www.ohchr.org/EN/ProfessionalInterest/Pages/CRC.aspx

4

SEPARATED, UNACCOMPANIED AND REFUGEE CHILDREN

AT A GLANCE THIS CHAPTER COVERS:

- entry to the UK and status of separated, unaccompanied and refugee children
- immigration and welfare systems support for separated or unaccompanied children and refugee children in families
- language and cultural differences and assessment of separated and unaccompanied children
- age disputes and access to welfare resources
- transitions between childhood and adulthood and exclusions from welfare
- triple-planning approach

In recent years local authorities have been widely criticized for failing to provide support for separated children and unaccompanied asylum-seeking children (UASCs), particularly with regard to accommodation and services when they reach 18. In this chapter the issues raised for social workers by the arrival into the UK of separated and unaccompanied children are discussed. The legal status and entitlements of children and young people coming to the UK are often politically charged because of the issues related to their illegal entry. Critiques of government policies towards separated and unaccompanied children coming to the UK suggest that, when it comes to balancing children's welfare and suspected illegal entry to the UK: 'the UK government has been overwhelmingly focused on the immigration control aspect' (Kvittingen, 2010:15).

The duties of local authorities to support separated and unaccompanied children and young people are clearly rooted in Article 22 UNCRC and in ss 17 and 20 Children Act 1989. Subsequent appeal court cases have been highly critical of local authorities who neglect their duties towards these children and young people, particularly when they reach the age of 18. It is not the remit of social workers or other child care/welfare professionals to judge the conditions or reasons why separated or unaccompanied children come to the UK. The role of the social worker is to ensure that their rights are respected whilst they are here and, importantly, that their needs are assessed and responded to. This chapter begins with an explanation of the definitions used and an overview of what we know about separated and unaccompanied children. The legislation which governs social work in this area and cases brought before the courts illustrate the responsibilities and duties of local authorities and social workers who play a key role ensuring that the needs of separated children and UASCs are addressed. This necessarily includes an understanding of the importance that the age assessment process plays and ensuring that age-disputed children are treated fairly. If a child is incorrectly assessed as being an adult, their entitlement to protection and support under international law is heavily compromised (Crawley et al., 2012).

Definition

The term separated children (Crawley et al., 2012:10) is used to define children (under 18) 'who are outside their country of origin and separated from their parent, legal or customary primary carer'. It must also be remembered that: 'Separation is a devastating experience for children and young people and can have serious long-term consequences for their well-being.' (Crawley et al., 2012:10) Separated children include those children who are accompanied by a relative or other adult who is unable or unwilling to care for them and abandons them when they arrive in the UK. Separated children are also those who travel to the UK for their safety, education and or health, with or without the consent of their parents. UASCs are those children and young people claiming asylum who are less than 18 years old and have come to the UK unaccompanied by parents or carers who would usually have responsibility for them (Crawley et al., 2012). Once these children arrive in the UK, general welfare, education, health and settlement needs can be marginalized as seeking asylum status and age determination takes priority:

> Children and young people experience, and are affected by, immigration control decisions and procedures in ways that are different from adults. They have often had little or no choice in the decisions that have led to their situation. Children and young people are particularly vulnerable to harm and require procedures appropriate to their age, level of maturity and individual needs. They are children first and migrants second. Regardless of a child or young person's immigration status, his or her best interests must always be of primary consideration.
>
> *Crawley et al., 2012:29*

Separated and unaccompanied children coming to the UK

Children coming to the UK are subject to regulations of the UKBA whether they arrive at a port of entry with or without valid documentation and claim asylum or whether they arrive through a clandestine entry. It almost goes without saying that children subject to immigration control will be anxious and fearful. Crawley et al. (2012) outline the key factors to consider when professionals from UKBA or other agencies come into contact with separated or unaccompanied children in interviews or other formal proceedings. Clearly, remaining child-centred is important as is ensuring that basic needs are met initially. The use of interpreters is also advocated. Crawley et al. (2012) remind us that the court considers the welfare of the child to be paramount, that delay might prejudice the welfare of the child and, in addition, children's wishes and feelings need to be taken into account in accordance with their age and understanding. In addition to the Children Act 1989, UK legislation relevant to separated children or UASCs includes the Children (Leaving Care) Act 2000 and s. 55 Borders, Citizen and Immigration Act 2009 which introduced a statutory duty on border agencies to ensure the well-being of children and young people coming to the UK.

Children and young people coming to the UK who do so to seek political protection are likely to have experienced or be at risk of persecution from their government or other local groups. This may involve physical threats to their life for several reasons including religious beliefs, forced national service or participation in criminal groups, land disputes, and being trafficked or sold into the sex trade. Children travel to the UK for family reunification as well as seeking protection from persecution, or searching for better living conditions, education and opportunities (Kohli, 2007; Nando and Hughes, 2012). These experiences, including the journey, make separated children and UASCs vulnerable and in need of support when they do arrive in the UK. These children often arrive without documents to evidence where they have travelled from, and without plans for their care when they arrive. According to Crawley (2010), children and young people arrive in the UK by chance rather than choice and few are involved in deciding to come to the UK – the destination being decided by their agent. Their arrival raises many concerns for statutory and safeguarding agencies at ports of entry and in some circumstances these concerns about risk of trafficking or safeguarding override prioritizing the duty to assess their needs (Westwood, 2012).

The best interests of the child are also a consideration in making decisions about removals of children, as *R(TS) v Secretary of State* [2010] illustrates (see page 73).

In August 2012, there were 1398 applications for asylum made by children and young people in the UK, a decrease since 2010. In 2011, 127 children and young people who came to the UK were held in detention. Most applications for asylum were from male children (Refugee Council, 2012b). The situations these children and young people find themselves in – having no status, requiring legal advice, potentially being detained and having no parent/carer to support them – clearly indicates that they are 'in need' as defined in s. 17 Children Act 1989. However, children's organizations and refugee/asylum charities have argued that the current system falls short of the ideal. The economic climate also has a bearing on resources available to meet these needs:

without sufficient resources it is hard to imagine how children who have endured traumatic departures and terrible journeys could begin to recover and come to terms with what has happened to them. There are particular resource and protection gaps as these children approach adulthood and lose their entitlement to support as children.

Maggie Atkinson, Children's Commissioner for England,
cited in Matthews, 2012:5

> **KEY CASE ANALYSIS**

R (TS) v Secretary of State for the Home Department and Another [2010]

In this case the High Court held that the UKBA had not given primary consideration to the best interests of the child when it had decided to remove a child asylum-seeker to Belgium for his asylum claim to be dealt with there. The child had been living in the UK for several months and become settled in the environment in which he was living. He suffered from post-traumatic stress disorder (PTSD) and required treatment for this. The High Court accepted Belgium would treat the child in accordance with international obligations (which it shares with the UK). However, the UKBA was required to consider what was best for the child, not simply whether Belgium would behave responsibly. Displacing the child from the social and educational environment to which he had become familiar would not be in his best interests and the UKBA had given no or no adequate consideration to this. The decision to remove the child to Belgium was unlawful.

The appeal was allowed because the need to safeguard and promote the claimant's welfare could not be established when it was decided that the claimant would be removed to Belgium. Whilst it was accepted that the claimant was suffering from PTSD and that it could be treated in Belgium, the claimant's doctor had argued that removal to Belgium would exacerbate the claimant's PTSD. The decision-maker had found that the claimant's medical condition was not so compelling as to warrant departure from the usual practice of removing. If that conclusion was wrong, in any event the decision-maker had not treated the best interests of the child as a primary consideration, since the decision letter had not begun to identify the reasons which would have permitted him to give less weight to the best interests of the claimant.

Age assessment

The Home Office has specific powers to determine age for the purpose of immigration, and yet no statutory or procedural guidance has been issued to local authorities. There have been criticisms of the way in which some local authorities have implemented age assessment processes and procedures (Bianchini, 2011). A set of practice guidance is outlined in Wise et al. (2011) which was developed by the London Boroughs of Croydon and Hillingdon. Both of these boroughs have ports of entry (Gatwick and Heathrow Airports) and are likely to see a disproportionate number of separated children and UASCs.

The way in which age assessments have become part of the process for judging the entitlement of children and young people to claim asylum in the UK has been criticized as it has been used to prevent access to welfare services which children and young people are entitled to (Kvittingen, 2010). Much hangs on the age assessment. It does not just determine whether a young person is under or over 18, it can have significant implications in terms of support and resources available, as well as protection under international law. A UASC assessed as under the age of 16 years will be entitled to care in a foster placement or residential home and access to other welfare resources such as clothing budgets, whereas a UASC assessed as being 16 or 17 is more likely to be placed into supported lodgings or shared accommodation properties without additional adult support (Crawley, 2012; Wright, 2012).

The weight given to medical methods of assessing age has also been challenged in *A v London Borough of Croydon and Secretary of State for the Home Department (Interested Party); and WK v Secretary of State for Home Department and Kent County Council* [2009]. The judge reviewed the evidence in 70 cases on age assessment from social workers, the processes used in local authorities and the Home Office, as well as the legal framework and the relevant paediatric reports, and found that, whilst it was important to take all reports into account, if there was a variance then this must be in the UASC's favour. Procedures in local authorities have thus developed through practice and legal challenges. In *R (on the Application of B) v Merton London Borough Council* [2003], the judge set down some guidelines in relation to age assessment of unaccompanied children and young people without documentary evidence to prove their age. This was reiterated in *R (AS) v London Borough of Croydon*

[2011]. A *Merton* compliant age assessment now provides a benchmark for conducting and evaluating social service age assessments.

There are clear difficulties in assessing ages which the *Merton* ruling does seek to address. However, it is also important to recognize that childhood is defined in different ways and, in many parts of the world, children's births are not officially registered. Some countries use a calendar system which is different from that in Europe, and as such children may not actually know how old they are. Finally, the experiences of childhood vary and responsibilities and hardships or trauma can make children appear older than their chronological years. Ethnic and developmental differences make it a difficult task to generalize about physical appearance/maturity being an age-determining factor. If an age assessment is required, good practice suggests that this should be undertaken by two social workers.

Merton compliant guidance

> **KEY CASE ANALYSIS**

R (on the Application of B) v Merton London Borough Council [2003]

This was a case which led to the *Merton* compliant guidance. In the case the child was unaccompanied and seeking asylum. The assessment process was criticized as inadequate: the claimant did not have support from an independent person during the assessment and the interpreter did not keep a record of the questions asked by the claimant during the assessment. It is fair to say that, when asylum cases such as these began to appear in local authorities, there was a lack of consistency in the application of adequate, fair and transparent assessment methods. The *Merton* guidance addresses this.

An assessment cannot be made solely on the basis of appearance, and should be an holistic one, taking account of the young person's appearance, demeanour, background and credibility. Any assessment should take into account relevant factors from the child's medical, family and social history, and the decision-maker should seek to elicit the general background of the applicant including his or her family circumstances and history, educational background and activities during the previous few years. Ethnic and cultural information may also be important. There was a duty on the decision-makers to give reasons for a decision that an applicant claiming to be a child is not a child. The young person should be given an opportunity during the assessment to answer any adverse points the decision-maker was minded to hold against them. Age assessments must be conducted by experienced trained social workers and all the safeguards to ensure fairness must be in place. If the decision-maker is left in doubt, the claimant should receive the benefit of that doubt.

On-the-spot question

1 How do you usually confirm the age of a child or young person you are assessing?
2 Reflect on what difficulties you may encounter in undertaking an age assessment of a child from a culture different from your own.

Children in families who are seeking asylum

The issues facing separated and unaccompanied children in terms of frequent moves, access to health and welfare, uncertainty of status and not being believed are also experiences facing children who come to the UK to seek asylum with their parents. In 2013, a cross-party inquiry reported on the situations of children in families where parents were seeking asylum and identified a range of issues which impacted on children's well-being generally. The panel heard evidence from young people and families who have experienced asylum support services, as well as refugee and asylum organizations, poverty and health experts, housing organizations, local councils, social workers and academics. Government ministers responsible for child poverty and immigration provided a written submission outlining the government's position:

> Although the inquiry's focus was on those in receipt of asylum support, the panel was shocked to hear of instances where children were left destitute and homeless, entirely without institutional support and forced to rely on food parcels or charitable donations … Frequent moves and failures on continuity of care, disruption to children's friendships, education and family support networks were also a profoundly negative influence on children's well-being. We were presented with evidence of the increased maternal and infant death rates amongst pregnant women in the asylum system, caused by poverty, problems accessing care and social isolation.
>
> *Children's Society, 2013:iii*

The inquiry made a series of recommendations which related to improving the asylum support process, addressing issues related to welfare and levels of income support, the disruption to home and school life of frequent moves owing to dispersal and the impact of these circumstances on health and well-being of children and their parents:

> What most concerned the panel was the host of problems encountered by children and families in the asylum support system who are moved with no regard to their education, relationships, health or home life. The lack of privacy and respect shown to asylum seekers reflects the pervasive attitude entrenched throughout the asylum support system that this group of children and families are less deserving than others.
>
> *Children's Society, 2013:24*

UASCs and the UNCRC

The UNCRC is an international human rights treaty which grants all children and young people a comprehensive set of rights. When the UK ratified the UNCRC it entered a reservation to allow it not to apply the Convention to decisions concerning children and young people subject to immigration control. This was removed in November 2008. As such, the UK government has accepted that all children irrespective of their immigration status, whether seeking to enter or remain in the UK, must enjoy all the rights and protections of the Convention without discrimination. The UN High Commission for Refugees (UNHCR) has published *Guidance on Determining the Best Interests of the Child* which contains information on what needs to be taken into account when identifying the best interests of separated, refugee and unaccompanied children seeking asylum (UNHCR, 2008). Factors which need to be considered include: safe environment; family and close relationships; and development and identity needs (Crawley et al., 2012).

Article 22(1) and (2) UNCRC is our starting point for understanding the rights of UASCs who arrive here. Essentially, this Article states that those unaccompanied children are to receive appropriate protection and humanitarian assistance and support for family tracing and reunification where this is possible. The Article also states that:

Article 22

> where no parents or other members of the family can be found, the child shall be accorded the same protection as any other child permanently or temporarily deprived of his or her family environment for any reason.
>
> *UNCRC*

Article 3 is one of the fundamental principles of the UNCRC which must be central to decision-making about separated or unaccompanied children or young people:

Article 3

> all actions concerning children and young people, whether undertaken by public or private social welfare institutions, courts of law, administrative authorities or legislative bodies, the best interests of the child shall be a primary consideration
>
> *UNCRC*

Separated children and young people are not able to be supported by their families and so must rely on the state for their care and welfare. These are children who are also vulnerable to harm and so require special protection measures which involve continuing assessment of their needs to ensure that their best interests are met whilst they are going through the asylum process and status determination. The best interest principle also means that children and young people subject to immigration control:

> need a timely resolution to their case and certainty about the future. The 'no delay' principle has long been integral to UK domestic children and family law. This principle is no less important than in other legal arenas involving children. Children and young people need a durable solution to the problems that affect their lives and their long-term immigration status should not be left undecided until they are approaching or have turned 18.
>
> *Crawley et al., 2012:34*

It is also important to ensure the child's right to participate in all decisions affecting him or her, directly or indirectly. Article 12 UNCRC states that every child has the right to express his or her views, opinions or beliefs freely in all matters, in his or her own words, and to contribute to the decisions affecting his or her life, including those taken in any judicial process and to have those views taken into consideration. The views of the child or young person should be given due weight, in accordance with the age and maturity of the child. Separated and unaccompanied children are entitled to participate in decision-making about them and it is thus incumbent on professionals working with them and on the organizations and agencies who provide services to ensure that they have systems in place to make this right a reality.

Detention

The UKBA policy is to not detain children, however, in certain circumstances separated children and young people are held in detention centres in the UK pending inquiries about their status, prior to entry to the UK or directly before their removal. A separated or unaccompanied child or young person subject to immigration control should never be detained simply because he or she has turned 18 and using detention as a form of immigration control is unlawful. Matthews (2012) reported on a study of unaccompanied children arriving in Dover. There were several issues related to the reception unaccompanied children received and particularly the practice of returning children to France, which the UKBA is now addressing. The standard set by Article 37(b) UNCRC and government policy that requires that children should only be detained as a measure of last resort and for the shortest appropriate period of time was not adhered to. The report found that children were being detained for the 'shortest appropriate period of time' but held whilst significant interviews were carried out, and these interviews were likely to have a bearing on the prospects of their being granted permission. The cases examined for the report suggested that that the local authority is only informed of the child's arrival several hours after initial detention and well into the interviewing process. The report recommended that this practice should cease. There were several issues reported in the study which suggest that practice at the port was not compliant with good practice guidance or with the UNCRC – a failure to have a responsible adult present during the screening interview, as well as difficulties in working with interpreters leading to miscommunication and inaccuracies. The overarching recommendation from the study was that an initial interview at the port of entry should only gather basic data and a further interview regarding their claim or status:

… should be postponed until after a child has had a period of some days (or longer if deemed necessary by a childcare professional) to recover from their journey, and so that they have the opportunity to instruct a legal representative (Matthews, 2012:10).

Detention of separated and unaccompanied children

Her Majesty's Inspectorate of Prisons inspected the short-term holding facilities at Heathrow Airport Terminals 3 and 4 in March 2011 and found that, in the three months to February 2011, 174 children has been detained, including 16 unaccompanied minors. The average lengths of detention were 8 hours 20 minutes (Terminal 3) and 9.9 hours (Terminal 4). Twenty-four children had been held for over 18 hours (across both terminals) and the longest periods of detention were just under 24 hours. He also observed a child being detained with his father at Terminal 4 without the necessary authority. The child was signed in as a 'visitor' and, consequently, his detention would not have been recorded. According to figures obtained in a freedom of information request made by the Children's Society, 697 children were detained between May and the end of August 2011 across all Greater London and South East ports – almost a third were unaccompanied children. The Children's Society was unable to obtain information on the length of or reasons for their detention (House of Commons Library, 2013).

The impact of detention on separated and unaccompanied children can be traumatic for them and research has found this consistently. In 2010, the Coalition government made a commitment to end the detention of children, however, short-term holding facilities at ports of entry remain and are routinely used by the UKBA to detain children. Where it is found that detention is used unlawfully by the UKBA, it will be open to legal challenge and claims for damages (Crawley et al., 2012).

Social work and separated children and UASCs

Children and young people who are separated or unaccompanied become clients of social care agencies and need accommodation under s. 20 Children Act 1989, which was reinforced by the *Hillingdon* judgment (*R (Behre and Others) v Hillingdon Borough Council* [2003]). Section 20 of the Act places a duty on a local authority to 'look after' a child in need, if they appear to need such a level of service. This involves consulting the child about a placement and a general duty to safeguard the welfare of the child. Section 20 also requires a local authority to provide a service to those leaving care. Up until the *Hillingdon* judgment, most UASCs received the lesser support under s. 17 Children Act 1989 (Refugee Council, 2005). In June 2003, the DH issued a local authority circular (DH, 2003) following an amendment to the Children Act 1989. This circular clarified government policy on the responsibilities of social services to separated and unaccompanied children and young people seeking asylum:

> … where a child has no parent or guardian in this country … the presumption should be that he would fall within the scope of section 20 (of the Children Act, 1989) and become looked after, unless the needs assessment reveals particular factors which would suggest that an alternative response would be more appropriate. While the needs assessment is being carried out, he should be cared for under section 20.
>
> *DH, 2003*

A separated child or UASC or young person who comes to the UK will almost certainly have initial contact with the UKBA. The duty under s. 55 Borders, Citizen and Immigration Act 2009 requires agencies to safeguard and promote the well-being of children coming to the UK, and in most cases this will necessitate a referral to social services. Once they are referred the child or young person becomes the responsibility of the local authority where they arrive into or where their place of abode is (if they have one). There is a duty (s. 17 Children Act 1989) to assess needs and to provide accommodation to children. If the child or young person is looked after or more commonly accommodated (s. 20 Children Act 1989), the social worker will undertake statutory reviews and visits to ensure that the care package is working. Once basic needs have been addressed and accommodation/care arranged, the social workers will support unaccompanied and asylum-seeking children and young people to access legal advice regarding their rights to claim asylum. The social worker may accompany the child or young person to interviews with the UKBA, and to any subsequent court hearings and provide support in relation to their culture and language issues. Many of these children and young people will have complex emotional needs and personal and family histories which may well feature loss and violence (Newbigging and Thomas, 2010).

On-the-spot question	What difficulties might there be for you in assessing the needs of a child or young person who has recently arrived from an occupied or invaded country?

UASCs and leaving care

Problematically, it is in this arena that the failings and disparities in provision to separated children and UASCs are most explicit as several local authorities have withdrawn support once the young person reaches the age of 18. This practice has been challenged in the appeal court. In *R (O) v London Borough of Barking and Dagenham and SSHD (The Children's Society Intervention)*, the court dealt with the appeal about whom the support of O (a care leaver) should fall to – the local authority or the National Asylum Support Service. The court found that,

---

PRACTICE FOCUS

Samia, aged 14, arrived in the UK as a refugee, without documents. She had been travelling over land for several months and at the port of entry the immigration officials disputed her age. The social worker was required to assess Samia's age and drew on the *Merton* guidance to inform the assessment. The social worker assessed that Samia was probably around the age of 14. Samia was given discretionary leave to remain until her 18th birthday.

Samia was accommodated under s. 20 Children Act 1989 in a local authority children's home; she attended school and is now attending a further education college and hoping to go on to university.

- What rights does Samia have to remain in the UK beyond 18?
- What is the likelihood of this?
- What support can the social worker draw on to assist Samia to claim the right to remain beyond her 18th birthday?
- Samia is anxious about using family tracing services as she thinks this will put other members of her family in her country of origin at risk. What assistance might be offered to Samia to maintain links with her family?
- Samia lost her appeal and cannot remain in the UK beyond her 18th birthday. What support and advice can the social worker offer Samia in this situation?

given that O was a care leaver, the local authority had a duty to continue support.

> The effect of this judgement is that such young people remain the responsibility of the local authority, and are unlikely to be eligible for asylum support because they will not be destitute. (Wise et al., 2011)

The specific issues related to care leavers and access to ongoing support once they leave care are discussed further in Chapter 6.

Legal status and leave to remain

Data collated by the Refugee Council find that the majority of decisions on asylum applications by unaccompanied children under the age of 17 are grants of discretionary leave. Discretionary leave to remain was introduced in 2003 and is given if the claimant is not recognized as a refugee or a person who qualifies for humanitarian protection. It is temporary permission to stay in the UK dependant on circumstances, but unlikely to be more than three years initially. It is only given in limited circumstances and applications for renewal will involve a review of circumstances (Home Office, 2012). In 2011, 48 per cent of all grants of discretionary leave were to children aged 17 and under. For decisions on unaccompanied children who have reached the age of 18 there was a refusal rate of 82 per cent in 2011(Refugee Council, 2012b). Wright (2012) notes that social workers who support separated and unaccompanied children report that there have been changes in the decisions for extensions to grants of discretionary leave since 2010. This has resulted in asylum-seeking young people being refused permission to stay in the UK once they are 18 years old. This emphasis in reduction is coupled with a push for returns and a financial saving for leaving care costs, a situation which poses difficulties for social workers in supporting young people. Wright (2012) argues that achieving a balance in promoting the best interests of children and young people is at odds with the UKBA's emphasis on pursuing their return to their country of origin.

Wright (2012) discusses the triple-planning approach which should be instigated once a separated child or UASC has been refused leave to remain or their entitlement to be in the UK is threatened by the end of their leave to remain when they reach the age of 18. This process starts with the pathway plan (discussed in Chapter 6) and covers three even-tualities. The first of these is that that there will be a removal requirement which will see the young person returned to their country of origin which is now deemed safe. The second assumption is that the young person will be granted the right to remain in the UK, and the third that they will remain without the entitlement.

This chapter provided an overview of the issues facing separated and unaccompanied children coming to the UK and how the legislation is designed to both assess need and determine their legal right of entry. The situations of children in families seeking asylum was also outlined. The barriers and restrictions imposed by immigration systems are keenly felt by separated and unaccompanied children who have limited power and autonomy in the asylum-seeking process on entry to the UK without advocates and legal representation. The UNCRC guides the way in which social work practice has evolved and various legal challenges have shaped the way in which local authorities respond to their duties under s. 17 Children Act 1989. As we will see in Chapter 6, the entitlement to leaving care provision for separated and unaccompanied children should be no different from those children born in the UK. This chapter also discussed how sensitive and informed assessment can also ensure that, where children and young people exhaust the appeal process and are required to return to their country of origin, this can be done in a safe and dignified manner.

Further reading

Coram Children's Legal Centre (2012) *Seeking Support: A Guide to the Rights and Entitlements of Separated Children.* Coram offers services, support and assistance for children and young people coming to the UK. It provides one-to-one advice, a range of free resources and information, and train-ing to professionals. This publication outlines the rights of refugee and migrant children in England, and provides advice to professionals on how to support young people in accessing those rights. Coram also advises that, as legislation and policy are subject to frequent change, practition-ers may wish to subscribe to the Migrant Children's Project newsletter for updates at www.childrenslegalcentre.com.

Crawley et al. (2012) *Working with Children and Young People Subject to Immigration Control: Guidelines for Best Practice* is an invaluable source of information for social work practitioners working in this area, providing detailed guidance on a range of interventions including interviewing, interpretation and age disputes. This updated resource covers the guidance and regulations as they relate to the four nations in the UK.

Fell, P and D Hayes (2007) *What Are They Doing Here? A Critical Guide to Asylum and Immigration* serves as a useful introductory text for UK professionals working with asylum-seekers and refugees and to social work students who are new to the area and wish to familiarize themselves with issues relevant to working with this client group.

Wright, F (2012) 'Social work practice with unaccompanied asylum-seeking young people facing removal' *British Journal of Social Work* 1–18 discusses the ways in which social workers support young people in the asylum system and subject to removal procedures, advocating an ecological assessment and intervention model which is child-centred and a triple-planning approach for those whose claims are rejected.

5

SOCIAL WORK AND CHILDREN WITH DISABILITIES

AT A GLANCE THIS CHAPTER COVERS:

- international and domestic legal framework related to children with disabilities
- complex multifaceted and changing needs of children with disabilities
- multi-professional work as key to assessing the needs of children with disabilities
- creativity in family support and intervention
- need for careful and long-term planning for transition to adulthood

Children with disabilities are singled out in s. 17(11)(c) Children Act 1989 as being *in need*. In practice services for disabled children are provided under the Chronically Sick and Disabled Persons Act 1970 (CSDPA) which has a more enforceable duty. The needs of children and their families and carers change over time and, whilst support might be focused on parents when children are very young, and should be multi-professional, the emphasis will inevitably shift towards a child-centred perspective as children grow older and their needs and development change. This chapter discusses the ways in which families and children with disabilities seek and access support and how these needs change and evolve. This chapter also examines the provisions in the Children Act 1989 for children who have disabilities, together with provisions specific to disability, such as those included in the CSDPA. The particular difficulties in the transition processes of disabled young people to adults' services and difficulties in supporting parents and carers during this transition are looked at together with some key examples of how legislation and policy have moved towards supporting and empowering families to care for their children and young people with disabilities and the inevitable tensions that are encountered in this.

Social work with children with disabilities and their families

It is difficult to determine how many children have a disability in the UK and there is a lack of quantitative data at a national level on prevalence and trends in terms of the numbers of children with disabilities. Data is collated by both local and national organizations for different purposes and there is a lack of standardization and categorization which would yield accurate data on the number of disabled children in the UK. What we can glean from the statistics suggests that the majority of disabled children live at home with their families (91 per cent) (Gordon et al., 2000, cited in Read et al., 2006) with the remainder being cared for by relatives, in foster care, or in residential care. There has been an increase in the numbers of disabled children being born with high levels of needs as technology and health care have improved, particularly for premature/low birthweight babies and those with multiple and/or complex disorders. Care for pre-term infants has improved and so children who may have not survived infancy a few decades ago are growing up and making the transition from childhood to adulthood. Society and families have adapted in response with the provision of home and community-based care. Children with complex disabilities require a great deal of support to meet their needs and are likely to be cared for at home by parents who are trained to use technologically innovative medical procedures (assisted ventilation, tube-feeding), mobility equipment (hoists) and to provide physiotherapy, and extended sessions of play and interaction to stimulate and promote their child's cognitive, physical and intellectual development.

Human rights, ethics and values are all important considerations in respect of social work practice with children with disabilities and their families. In working to achieve equality of opportunity for disabled children it is important to use research, theory, and legislation (Read et al., 2006). The starting assumption is that children with disabilities and their families are entitled to the same experiences and opportunities as others. In addition, there is a widespread commitment to personalization and empowerment of families and their children to decide on the care package which would best suit them. Research and reports from inspections of services for children with disabilities, however, consistently find that disabled children and their families face multiple forms of discrimination and barriers to participation. There is a strong likelihood that problems occur between care providers, funders and families in relation to the ongoing and changing/evolving care needs of children with disabilities and the support needs of families to continue caring. This becomes difficult when parents and children are not merely the recipients of the services they need but also in effect the purchasers.

There are several aspects of care which require careful consideration. The legal framework provides for a range of circumstances and eventualities and it is essential that social workers are able to draw on the legislation and practice guidance to promote the best interests of these children and their families. It is also crucial that social workers recognize the changing and evolving needs of children with disabilities and respond to these in a planned way which is respectful of the rights of the family and the child to access services they need.

Children with disabilities and the UNCRC

There is an expanding range of domestic and international sources of law affecting disabled children and their families. As outlined in Chapter 3, the ECHR was incorporated into UK domestic law through the HRA. The most relevant Article in respect of disabled children and their families is Article 8 ECHR, the right to respect for family, home and private life. The UNCRC has also made a significant contribution to improving the rights of children with disabilities.

The UNCRC creates a host of basic rights which should be enjoyed by all children. The following are particularly relevant to children with disabilities: Article 2 UNCRC deals with non-discrimination; Article 3 UNCRC the best interests of the child; Article 4 UNCRC maximizing resources for children to achieve rights; Article 12 UNCRC the right to participation; Article 23 UNCRC the right to a full and decent life; and Article 24 UNCRC the right to achieve the highest standard of health.

As discussed in Chapter 3, a children's rights perspective alerts us to the potential contributions which children and young people can make to defining the issues which they face. This is certainly the case when it comes to understanding the perspectives of children with disabilities. It is not sufficient to simply rely in any context on the adults who care for their child to speak for the child and, consequently, consultation with and the participation of children with disabilities should be given the highest priority alongside valuing the contributions from parents and carers in all aspects of assessment and review processes, and in regard to consent (Read et al., 2006).

Article 23 UNCRC requires states to recognize that disabled children should enjoy 'full and decent' lives and the right of disabled children to 'special care'. Such support is to be provided to disabled children free of charge where possible, subject to resources. The aim of such support should be to allow every child to achieve 'the fullest possible social integration and individual development'.

In June 2009 the UK ratified the UN Convention on the Rights of Persons with Disabilities 2006 (Disability Convention). Article 3 Disability Convention outlines the general principles, including respect for inherent dignity and for full and effective participation and inclusion in society. Article 7 Disability Convention relates specifically to disabled children and requires states to: 'Take all necessary measures to ensure the full enjoyment by children with disabilities of all human rights and fundamental freedoms on an equal basis with other children.' Article 7(2) Disability Convention reinforces the Article 3 UNCRC requirement that, in all actions concerning a disabled child, the child's best interests shall be a primary consideration. Similarly, Article 7(3) Disability Convention reinforces the right to participation under Article 12 UNCRC, and requires states to help disabled children realize this right. Article 9 Disability Convention deals with accessibility and Article 19 with independent living and inclusion in the community. Article 23(3) Disability Convention specifically requires that disabled children have equal rights in respect of family life, and requires states to provide 'early and comprehensive information, services and support' to prevent 'concealment, abandonment, neglect and segregation' of disabled children. Under Article 23(5) Disability Convention, where the immediate family is unable to care for a disabled child, the state must try to find alternative care within the extended family or in the community.

Article 24 Disability Convention concerns education and it requires states to establish an 'inclusive education system'. The UK has stated its definition of inclusion as being committed to continuing to develop an inclusive system. Disabled people have a right to be educated 'on an equal basis with others in the communities in which they live' (Article 24(2)(b) Disability Convention). The UK has a reservation in regard to Article 24 which reserves the right for disabled children to be educated outside their local community if there is appropriate education provision elsewhere. Parents of disabled children are, however, still able to state a preference for the school where they wish their child to be educated (Broach et al., 2010).

UK guidance and legislation related to children with disabilities and their families

Statutory guidance is issued under a specific statutory provision, most frequently in relation to disabled children under s. 7 LASSA. Section 2 CSDPA creates specific duties to provide services 'ordinarily resident in the local authorities' area' and this includes disabled children, in relation to whom the local authority has functions under Part III Children Act 1989. The provision of services is not solely the responsibility of the local authority; indeed, in regard to children with disabilities, multi-agency provision is essential. Where a child is disabled, then an assessment carried out under the Children Act 1989 should determine whether a child is eligible for support under the CSDPA and ensure that families are provided with support to continue to care for their children (Wise et al., 2011). Section 17(11) Children Act 1989 defines a child with disabilities as follows:

s. 17(11)

… a child is disabled if he is blind, deaf or dumb or suffers from mental disorder of any kind or is substantially and permanently handicapped by illness, injury or congenital deformity or such other disability as may be prescribed.

Children Act 1989

Notwithstanding the outdated language, which lacks reference to the social model of disability, the definition is broad and thus includes a range of conditions and impairments including mental illness, learning and physical disability, attention deficit and hyperactivity disorder (ADHD), Asperger's syndrome and autism, for example. Where local authorities impose eligibility criteria and exclusion from assessment, for example, of children with ADHD, this is likely to be unlawful and discriminatory under the Equality Act 2010. Section 27 Children Act 1989 provides for one local authority to ask another authority or body (i.e. primary care trust (PCT), housing) to assist them in carrying out their functions and authorities receiving such a request have a duty to comply. The local authority also has a duty to maintain a register of disabled children (Schedule 2, para. 2, Children Act 1989). This is used for statistical purposes and for planning services. Parents may choose not to place their child on the register, but this does not then preclude them from accessing services or the entitlement of their child to an assessment.

On-the-spot question	Which department of your local authority maintains the register of disabled children?

Section 10 Children Act 2004 emphasizes the requirement that children's services authorities make arrangements to cooperate with their partners, which includes all the local health agencies. The aim of these cooperative arrangements must be to improve the well-being of children. The resource question between health and social care providers is, however, a concern for parents who need respite or support and the social worker plays an important role in terms of understanding the needs of children and their parents/carers and drawing on the resources and services required as part of the implementation of a package of support.

> **KEY CASE ANALYSIS**

R (T and Others) v Haringey London Borough Council [2005] EWHC 2235

The tensions between health, social care and education in relation to resourcing support for children with disabilities have on occasion led to legal challenges. This issue was considered in *R (T and Others) v Haringey London Borough Council*. The child, who was three years old, had a tracheotomy fitted at birth. Her mother was trained to provide appropriate care, which involved suctioning three times a night and the availability of a carer to deal with the tube if it became disconnected which happened frequently and occasioned the risk of death within minutes. The PCT provided 20 hours' respite care per week by qualified nurses. Various assessments indicated that further respite provision should be given. Whilst the local authority accepted that additional provision was required, it argued that this was a health service and therefore the responsibility of the PCT. Meanwhile the PCT argued that the local authority had the power to provide the service. Relevant factors included in this case were that the purpose of the respite care, which might be considered social care, was to provide medical care. The consequences of a failure in care emphasized the medical as opposed to the social service nature of the provision and it had in fact been provided by qualified and trained nurses previously. It was also concluded that the local authority had no duty to provide the respite care under ss 2 and 28A CSDPA because this did not extend to medical treatment.

The matter was subsequently resolved out of court. However, the case illustrates, firstly, that parents who care for their disabled children require support to do so and, secondly, that there are duties and powers within the legislation to ensure that this is provided by several agencies. There is tension and disagreement between agencies as to who has responsibility for providing support for families and assessment of needs should be seen as an ongoing process as children's conditions and needs change.

Mental Capacity Act 2005

The Mental Capacity Act 2005 applies to people over 16 in the UK and so includes children, who are those under the age of 18 years. The Act provides the legal framework for acting and making decisions on behalf of individuals who lack the mental capacity to make decisions for themselves. Those who work with or care for a person over the age of 16 must comply with these rules which apply whether the decisions are about life-changing events or everyday matters. The Act's starting point is the presumption of capacity:

s. 1

(2) A person must be assumed to have capacity unless it is established that he lacks capacity.

Mental Capacity Act 2005

The Act also states that people must be given all appropriate help and support to enable them to make their own decisions or to maximize their participation in any decision-making process.

s. 1

(3) A person is not to be treated as unable to make a decision unless all practicable steps to help him to do so have been taken without success.
(4) A person is not to be treated as unable to make a decision merely because he makes an unwise decision.
(5) An act done or decision made, under this Act for or on behalf of a person who lacks capacity must be done, or made, in his best interests.
(6) Before the act is done, or the decision is made, regard must be had to whether the purpose for which it is needed can be as effectively achieved in a way that is less restrictive of the person's rights and freedom of action.

Mental Capacity Act 2005

People who lack capacity are defined in s. 2:

s. 2

(1) For the purposes of this Act, a person lacks capacity in relation to a matter if at the material time he is unable to make a decision for himself in relation to the matter because of an impairment of, or a disturbance in the functioning of, the mind or brain.

Mental Capacity Act 2005

There may be instances when decisions about a child's property or finances need to be made if the child lacks capacity to make such decisions within s. 2(1) of the Act and is likely to still lack capacity to make financial decisions when they reach the age of 18. When assessing their best interests, the person providing care or treatment must consult those involved in the child/young person's care and anyone interested in their welfare – if it is practical and appropriate to do so. This may include the young person's parents. Care should be taken so as not to unlawfully breach the young person's right to confidentiality.

Sometimes there will be disagreements about the care, treatment or welfare of a young person aged 16 or 17 who lacks capacity to make relevant decisions. Depending on the circumstances, the case may be heard in the family courts or the Court of Protection. The Court of Protection may transfer a case to the family courts, and vice versa. This means that the choice of court will depend on what is appropriate in the particular circumstances of the case. For example, if the parents of a 17-year-old who has profound learning difficulties cannot agree on the young person's residence or contact, it may be appropriate for the Court of Protection to deal with the disputed issues as any orders made under the Children Act 1989 will expire on the young person's 18th birthday.

In *B (A Local Authority) v AM* the judge considered the case for considering an application for a care order in respect of a young person aged 16 or over with lifelong disabilities and whether it should be transferred to the Court of Protection to be dealt with under the Mental Capacity Act 2005 rather than the Children Act 1989. The child was aged 17 and had a diagnosis of severe learning disability, autism and severe Tourette syndrome and was not expected to be able to live independently. She would always require a high level of support from the adults around her to ensure that her needs were met. There were clear disagreements between the local authority and the mother of B relating to the care she was receiving and the potential disruptions to this. The case was dealt with at the Court of Protection and the following questions were considered:

- Is the child over 16?
- Does the child manifestly lack capacity in respect of the principal decisions which are to be made under the Children Act 1989?
- Are the disabilities giving rise to the lack of capacity lifelong or long-term?
- Can the decisions which arise in respect of the child's welfare all be taken and all issues resolved during the child's minority?
- Are the Court of Protection's powers or procedures more appropriate to resolve the outstanding issues?
- Can the child's welfare needs be fully met by those powers?

The judge found that AM's needs could be met by this process and ordered that the parties should try to resolve the care plan for AM outside of the court and should only return to court if there was a serious problem which could not be resolved. In this case the Court of Protection process addressed the issues meaningfully and swiftly, upholding the rights and best interests of AM to receive appropriate care, have regular contact with her family and have a Guardian appointed until she was 18.

Caring for children with disabilities

Parents, particularly mothers, tend to assume the primary responsibility for the care and support of children with disabilities and especially so for the prolonged nature of intimate and personal care. Fathers too play a significant role and are a main source of support for mothers in two-parent headed households, although in the general population there are more lone parents with disabled children (Beresford 1995, cited in Read et al., 2006). It also tends to be mothers who play a key role in terms of liaison with health and social care services. The career options for mothers are limited as there is a lack of suitable child care for disabled children and males who work report that their work is affected by taking time off. Siblings are also affected in relation to being required to assist parents with care or support tasks for their disabled sibling. The care of a disabled child requires a commitment and dedication from parents that far exceeds that usually required by parents in both volume and role and many everyday activities require careful planning and organizing, as well as transport. These challenges continue as children get older and require different levels of care and support. In addition, the informal reciprocal networks which families develop (babysitting and schoolfriend play dates) are more difficult to arrange when the child is disabled. It is challenging for parents to care for a child with disabilities and the Children Act 1989 recognizes this in relation to providing support for them as children in need.

R v London Borough of Lambeth (Respondents) ex parte W (FC) (Appellant) [2003] concerned a family which was housed by the London Borough of Lambeth but the accommodation was not suitable for the needs of two of the three children in the family as they were autistic, had severe learning difficulties and required constant supervision. The family was accommodated in a ground floor, two-bedroom, local authority flat, close to a road, with no garden or outside play area. The two disabled children were prone to run out of the front door and climb out of windows. The accommodation, it was argued, posed severe disadvantages to the children's health and well-being. Assessment of the needs of the children under the Children Act 1989 suggested that the family needed to be rehoused away from the road, to have a safe outside play area and to have four bedrooms. The challenge by the mother about the decision of the council as the housing authority was, however, abandoned and the mother then sought an order compelling the council to find and provide suitable accommodation in line with the children's assessed needs. Both the judge and the Court of Appeal held that the court has no power to intervene and rehouse the family even though it was 'less than satisfactorily treated' by Lambeth council. This is because the duty to assess and provide support to promote the welfare of children does not extend to individual children. The local authority had accepted A's priority need for rehousing, but suitable accommodation had not yet been found. The case presented did not justify the conclusion that either the social services department or the housing department of the local authority had unreasonably failed to exercise any of the relevant powers available to them. The case presented was that the council was under a mandatory duty under s. 17(1) Children Act 1989 to provide accommodation to the family in accordance with the assessed needs of the autistic children.

> **KEY CASE ANALYSIS**

LBH (A Local Authority) v KJ and Others [2007]

In this case, the child had suffered neonatal injuries in the form of some intercranial haemorrhaging. The consequence of which is that she had microcephaly, four-limb bilateral spastic cerebral palsy with visual impairment and severe learning difficulties. She was unable to move or even sit up unaided; she had no intelligible speech and required feeding directly by gastrostomy tube. In short she needed high levels of long-term personal care and would always be dependent on others for all her needs, including the most intimate personal care. Her mother was effectively a single parent with only a limited command of the English language. She had four other children at home and was pregnant. She was living in accommodation which was hopelessly inadequate. It had sleeping accommodation accessible only by stairs which meant that the child had to either live down-stairs or be physically carried upstairs. There was no bathroom on the ground floor which meant that the child's personal hygiene was dependent on bed baths. The accommodation was too small to install some basic equipment to help with moving and lifting.

These obstacles to care were compounded because the mother found it impossible to acknowledge that the care of her daughter could sometimes simply be too much for her and that she needed both help and respite. The mother had a difficult relationship with professionals, not taking their advice or keeping appointments. The mother was later admitted to hospital suffering from tuberculosis and the local authority placed the child in a residential unit, despite the opposition of the mother.

The judge reviewed whether the care the mother was able to give was inadequate and likely to cause significant harm to the child and found that the threshold criteria were reached, but not before making some interesting remarks on attributability and reasonable care. It was also noted that it cannot be right that a parent automat-ically falls foul of the threshold criteria where the local authority has not provided the support that could be expected, especially in the face of trying to care for a severely disabled child. There were very real concerns in the case that the mother had not received adequate support from the local authority when the child had been returned home for a few days, and concerns that the child had suffered and would continue to be at risk of significant harm. There were also several cultural and communication factors which made this case complex. It was stated in the discussion of the case that, whilst it was generally accepted that the best place for a disabled child to be brought up is in their family, there would undoubtedly be a tension in promoting the maximum achievement for them alongside the other demands of family life. The court, whilst accepting that the mother had failed to care adequately for her child, found that she had been compromised in her ability to do this by inadequate hous-ing provision.

The judge in this case noted several factors which are useful learn-ing points for social work practice in cases where a child is severely disabled. A whole-life approach to planning is important. This approach recognizes that the child will need not only care but some-one to take decisions for her indefinitely and the important role that the family – and especially siblings – might play in ensuring consis-tency in this regard.

Care planning then should make provision for the fullest involvement of the family (consistent of course with welfare) on the basis that they may well be involved in making decisions about a child's care as the child gets older. There should also be an acceptance that people have the capacity to change and, in this case, the judge believed that the mother was beginning to understand what was necessary for her to learn and had begun to cooperate. In this case it was thought that the resources which could support the mother to care for her child would facilitate the on-going development of that cooperation.

There are three major pieces of legislation which are relevant to the issues of caring for disabled children. The Carers (Recognition and Services) Act 1995 outlines the statutory responsibilities and the carer's assessment, which was a new concept. If requested, the social services department will carry out a separate assessment of a carer when it assesses the needs of a disabled child. It also recognizes that there may be more than one carer in a household. The Carers and Disabled Children Act 2000 provides for the rights of carers and their entitlements to support services, including direct payments and vouchers. This was designed to provide for those who cared for people over 16. It ensures that carers are entitled to an assessment even if the cared for person has refused an assessment. It also made available services to carers to assist them with their caring responsibilities. The Carers (Equal Opportunities) Act 2004 introduced a statutory obligation on social services to inform carers of their rights and ensure that carers are advised of work, education/training and leisure opportunities. There is also a requirement for local authorities to ensure that there are sufficient and specific child care services available as detailed in the Childcare Act 2006. This Act requires English and Welsh local authorities to secure, 'so far as is reasonably practicable', sufficient child care to meet the needs of parents of disabled children in their area who require child care in order to work or to undertake training or education to prepare for work.

The Breaks for Carers of Disabled Children Regulations 2011 outline the duty to make provision for carers in regard to respite care. This recognizes that carers need breaks, support and access to training and education in order to continue to be able to provide the intensive and demanding care their children need:

s. 3

(2) … have regard to the needs of those carers who would be unable to continue to provide care unless breaks from caring were given to them.
…

(3) … have regard to the needs of those carers who would be able to provide care for their disabled child more effectively if breaks from caring were given to them to allow them to—
  (a) undertake education, training or any regular leisure activity,
  (b) meet the needs of other children in the family more effectively, or
  (c) carry out day to day tasks which they must perform in order to run their household.

Breaks for Carers of Disabled Children Regulations 2011

Decisions regarding the treatment of severely disabled children

Where children are severely disabled and have deteriorating conditions, parents and caregivers may have to seek permission from the court regarding the discontinuation of treatment. In *Re KH (A Child)* [2012], such a case was presented. KH received medical treatment and daily care of the very highest quality and there was no plan in place to withdraw this. What was being examined by the court was a decision being made which would not escalate treatment when his condition inevitably deteriorated. The escalation of treatment was not considered in his interests by his doctors, his carers or by his parents and it was agreed that treatment would not escalate as his condition deteriorated, however, treatment would be applied which would reduce pain and distress. These are difficult decisions to make and rightly are brought before the court.

The judge was minded to consider what was in KH's best interest. His parents had difficulties of their own and lacked the capacity to make decisions about KH's medical treatment. The case was brought by the NHS trust which wanted to seek agreement that treatment should not be escalated when the child's condition inevitably deteriorated, as this was not considered in his interests by his doctors, his carer, or his parents.

The advanced care plan was stated as follows:

- In the case of severe respiratory compromise, not to receive mouth-to-mouth or bag and mask resuscitation, endotracheal intubation, or invasive or non-invasive ventilation.
- In the event of cardiac arrest, not to receive cardiac resuscitation, including defibrillation, cardiac massage or resuscitation drugs including inotropes.
- In the event of serious infection, including pneumonia, not to undergo blood sampling or to receive intravenous antibiotics unless it is considered that such treatment would help to make him more comfortable and/or distress and pain free.
- In the event of deterioration in his gastro-oesophageal reflux, not to undergo a definite surgical procedure unless it is considered that such surgery would help to make him more comfortable and/or distress and pain free.
- In the event of deterioration of his medical condition, to receive pain medication (such as Morphine) and/or sedation (such as Midazolam) with the purpose of relieving suffering and distress, even though such medications might reduce his respiratory drive and thereby shorten his life.

The court considered whether the plan for KH's future medical treatment as described in the advanced care plan was in his best interests. The court also had to weigh up the advantages and disadvantages of providing or withholding the various treatment options within that plan when considering what was in KH's best interests. In making the decisions, the court had to exercise independent and objective judgment on the basis of all the available evidence. Finally, the court's approach to KH's best interests was necessarily fact-specific and had to focus on this child in this situation. Put simply, the complex and moral basis of decisions made about such treatment plans for severely disabled children with deteriorating conditions requires the same in-depth considerations as decisions given to children who are expected to live long lives.

On-the-spot question

1 How would you support a family which was caring for a child with a deteriorating condition?
2 Which articles of the UNCRC and the Disability Convention might need to be considered in a case like this?

Assessment of children with disabilities

> **KEY CASE ANALYSIS**

R (LH and MH) v London Borough of Lambeth [2006]

LH lived with his mother. He had autism, moderate learning difficulties, chronic long-term constipation, severe epilepsy and asthma. LH had an SEN statement and attended a specialist school for children with moderate or severe learning difficulties. The local authority was advised that LH's mother was struggling to cope with his behaviour at home. At a professionals' meeting, it was agreed that a core assessment was needed and that a residential placement, jointly funded by the education and social services departments, should be seriously considered. The core assessment stated that LH's mother was doing her best to meet his needs, but had difficulty coping with his challenging behaviour, and this was having an impact on her physical and mental health. The recommendation from the social worker was that LH's needs could be met in a boarding school which had already assessed his needs. However, this recommendation was not taken forward. Instead, in a meeting of the Social Services and Education Panel another core assessment was requested. The same social worker completed the assessment, which this time recommended parenting support for LH's mother. LH and his mother applied for judicial review of the revised core assessment claiming that the local authority was in breach of its obligation to complete its care plan. They claimed that the recommendation that a 'parenting' programme for his mother would meet LH's needs was irrational and lacked evidence and that the local authority had failed in its statutory obligations to consider the educational, health and social care interests of LH. The second core assessment was criticized by the judge for not focusing on the needs of LH.

The judge had to decide whether the local authority had failed to fulfil its legal obligations. In this instance, the proposal by the local authority to recommend a package of support instead of the residential placement was found to be seriously flawed and, in the circumstances, irrational. The judge in LH's case granted a declaration that the local authority had breached its assessment obligations under Part III Children Act 1989, as supplemented by the Children Act 2004, the Carers (Recognition and Services) Act 1995 and the Carers and Disabled Children Act 2000.

LH's case illustrates that social work assessments and decision-making are subject to judicial scrutiny if they are not undertaken with the purpose of meeting the needs of the child and in the child's best interests. The judge was critical of the local authority's second core assessment which had identified that a package of support was sufficient to meet LH's needs without properly defining what was included in this package.

> *On-the-spot question*
>
> What legislation and guidance would influence and inform your assessment of needs for a child with disabilities who was presenting with challenging behaviour?

Education and children with disabilities

The Education (Handicapped Children) Act 1970 ended the classification of some disabled children as 'unsuitable for education in school'. The Council of Europe has education as a 'basic instrument of social integration' for disabled children and this right is contained in a number of international treaties including Article 26 Universal Declaration of Human Rights, Article 13 International Covenant on Economic, Social and Cultural Rights, Articles 28 and 29 UNCRC and Article 24 Disability Convention. Article 2 Protocol 1 ECHR states that 'no-one shall be denied the right to education' and this means an 'effective education' in accordance with the education system 'prevailing in the state'.

The statutory scheme for children with SEN in England and Wales is set out in Part IV Education Act 1996, as amended by the Special Educational Needs and Disability Act 2001. This scheme is contained in several regulations, which detail the requirements for statutory assessments and statements of SEN and by a Special Educational Needs Code of Practice issued by the DfES in England (effective from 1 January 2002) and by the National Assembly for Wales (effective from 1 April 2002). The code of practice is statutory guidance issued under s. 313 Education Act 1996 which states on its face that Local Education Authorities (LEAs), schools, early education settings and other relevant bodies must have regard to it. LEAs have the overall responsibility for making sure that children's SEN are met.

Support for families and children with disabilities

Local authorities' duty to provide services pursuant to s. 2 CSPDA was considered in two cases. In *R (Spink) v Wandsworth Borough Council*

[2005], it was held that the local authority could charge for services (s. 29 Children Act 1989) that it had a duty to provide under (s. 2 CSPDA). In another case, *R (BG) v Medway District Council* [2005], the judge found that it was reasonable for the local authority to require repayment of a loan for adaptations if the child no longer resided there or died.

PRACTICE FOCUS

Malik is 12 and has lived with his grandparents, who are in their mid-60s, since he was four; he is accommodated under s. 20 Children Act 1989. Malik has severe learning and physical disabilities and requires full-time care for all of his personal needs. Malik attends a school for children with severe disabilities and has one night respite in a residential centre every week and one weekend a month. He has regular contact with his mother and siblings who live close by but he is not able to live with them.

The sheltered accommodation the grandparents rent from the local authority is proving to be inadequate as Malik is getting older. Malik has to be carried from one room to the next as the doorways cannot accommodate his wheelchair. He also has to be carried in and out of the house as there are steps which are too difficult to negotiate with a wheelchair. The hoists provided to get Malik in and out of the bath are too awkward to erect in the small bathroom and so Malik is washed on the floor of the bathroom and physically lifted in and out of bed. Malik's' grandparents wish to continue to care for their grandson but are struggling to cope with the physical demands; they are worried that they will have to put Malik into full-time residential care. What assistance might the local authority provide to support the grandparents?

Malik's grandparents and the social worker wrote to the local authority housing office outlining their struggles. After several months of correspondence, the housing officer visited the grandparents' home with a view to making some modifications using the disabled facilities grant, but found that the house was unsuited to any renovations.

A nearby housing association complex for disabled people was being developed during this time and the social worker supported the grandparents to apply for a new house on this scheme, and they were successful. The new accommodation had an en-suite bathroom for Malik, wide doorways and ramps for Malik's wheelchair as well as other adaptations to promote his independence.

Other services provided by the local authority might include practical assistance in the home, short breaks based in the community or in the child's home, practical assistance for recreational or educational facilities, holiday clubs or after-school activities. If a short break cannot be provided in the child's home then this would be provided outside of the home under either s. 7(6) or s. 20(4) Children Act 1989. Additionally, children with disabilities may require assistance to travel to/from an educational provision, and require support and/or personal care. The educational provision will also need to have suitable facilities for children with disabilities which is provided for under the Further and Higher Education Act 1992 and required under the Equality Act 2010.

Transition planning for children with disabilities

Although education has the lead responsibility, transition planning must be a multi-agency process. The regulations require that social services departments and other agencies should contribute to the transition plan. Section 5 Disabled Persons (Services, Consultation and Representation) Act 1986, states that the LEA must seek information from adult social services during the transition-planning process so as to determine whether a young person is likely to require adult social services assistance. Health bodies should also ensure that their adult NHS continuing healthcare unit is appropriately represented at all transition-planning meetings relating to disabled young people whose needs suggest that there may be potential eligibility for adult NHS continuing healthcare funding.

Transition to adulthood involves changes in the law and the service provision for children and young people with disabilities. The duties remain for disabled young people to have their needs assessed and services provided to meet these needs and this requires a multi-agency approach. Education authorities should take the lead in transition planning unless there has been significant social care or health input previously. Education authorities should develop a transition plan at the time of the annual review of the child's SEN statement at age 14. The statutory basis for the provision of social care continues under s. 2 CSDPA. However, this may not be the case for residential care which will change at age 18. Any assessments carried out to determine eligibility at 18 need to take into account earlier assessments. Where children and young people with disabilities have been accommodated by the local authority they are entitled to a personal advisor and pathway plan under the leaving care legislation (see Chapter 6). The transition from child to adult health services can be disruptive and careful planning is needed. The Mental Capacity Act 2005 also applies here to ensure that that the capacity of young people to make decisions is assessed. If it is found that decisions have to be taken on behalf of the young person, they must be in the young person's best interests.

This chapter began with a discussion of some of the difficulties there are in quantifying how many children with disabilities there are in the UK. This has an implication for planning services to meet needs, particularly in a context where medical advances improve the likelihood of the longer-term survival of disabled children. There have been huge developments in the last few decades which have promoted the rights and interests of disabled people generally and children with disabilities specifically, and the UK government has committed to ensuring that these rights are extended to carers. Whilst there are difficulties with multi-agency work in terms of communication and questions and legal disputes related to access to resources, working across health, education and social care services is vital to meet the holistic and evolving needs of children with disabilities. Cases discussed have raised serious issues about assessment and the provision of services to families to enable and support them to continue caring for their children. Finally. this chapter highlighted that the divide between children's and adult services is clearly artificial when it comes to meeting the needs of children with disabilities and their families. Disruptions to care packages because of organizational boundaries can have detrimental effects on children with disabilities and their families and careful detailed planning is key to preventing this throughout and beyond the transition period.

Further reading

Broach, S, L Clements and J Read (2010) *Disabled Children: A Legal Handbook*. The materials in this book provide a guide to the rights of disabled children and their families in England and Wales. The authors identify and explain the many sources of law, clarifying what local authorities must do to support disabled children and what they may do. It is a valuable text which is designed to empower disabled children and their families in relation to their rights and entitlements and is an essential text for the professionals working in this area and for students and academics. This authoritative and accessible legal handbook is also available online: www.councilfordisabledchildren.org.uk/resources/cdcs-resources/disabled-children-a-legal-handbook.

Joseph Rowntree Foundation (2008) *Housing and Disabled Children* provides details about the impact of housing issues for disabled children and their families.

Read, J, L Clements and D Ruebain (2006) *Disabled Children and the Law: Research and Good Practice*. This is a comprehensive text which discusses research and law as it relates to children with disabilities and their families. As well as identifying problems with data collection and promoting a disability perspective, this book explores the common legal obstacles affecting children with disabilities and covers various stages of development from the early years through to transition to adulthood. The appendices contain resources and materials for practitioners and parents to assist them in navigating their way through access to services for children with disabilities.

6

YOUNG PEOPLE LEAVING CARE

Children are 'looked after' in the UK in several ways. They may be accommodated under s. 20 Children Act 1989, a voluntary arrange-ment, or they may be looked after under a s. 31 Care Order which is made by application to the court. Other orders, under s. 8 Children Act 1989, may determine with whom a child or young person lives. Whichever applies, children will be looked after in foster care, residen-tial care, in detention or secure accommodation, or in respite care. Once children and young people reach the age of 16 in the UK they can legally leave home and this also applies to young people who are looked after. Once young people have left care they remain 'in need'. Research has consistently identified that young people who leave care are disadvantaged on several measures. Children who come into the care system are not living with their families because illness, poverty or overwhelming problems mean that parents can no longer look after their child.

Most children in care are with foster families rather than in residential care: those who live in children's homes now usually share with only four or five children, rather than living in large institutions. Many young people come through the care system and go on to live successful family lives. For some, this will include being permanently reunited with their birth families. For others, having foster carers and social work support can make all the difference to their lives. However, there remains a gap in achievement and aspirations between children in care and their peers (Who Cares Trust, 2014).

This chapter discusses how the law applies to young people leaving the care system. The experiences of young people leaving care and the support they receive from the state have been the subject of public and political scrutiny in recent years. Research studies highlight failings in local authority provision and cases brought before the appeal courts illus-trate the importance of social workers in this area having a clear under-standing of the local authority duties and responsibilities towards care leavers.

The policy emphasis for children and young people who leave care is on their achieving independence and, whilst this is clearly an important issue for children and young people who have been in the care system, research suggests that young people leaving care are not very well prepared for independence (Wade and Dixon, 2006) and have poorer outcomes in terms of health and well-being (Dixon, 2008) and educa-tion (Stein, 2006). The transition to adult services is not always effective or appropriate and this results in care leavers having limited support once they leave care (Wade, 2008). Indeed, whilst care leavers would argue they have a right to independence, the way in which they perceive and then experience independence is greatly at odds with their needs and capacities.

Research has demonstrated that leaving care is a complex process which requires careful planning, review and cooperation and support from agencies involved with the young person and their family (Wade, 2008). Care leavers often move to independence at a younger age than the general population (Wise et al., 2011). This is a worrying as young people who leave care do so often without the continued support of family which is available to other young people (Wade, 2008). Whilst for most people leaving home is a gradual process, with opportunities to return for temporary periods, this option is often not available for young people leaving care who will find themselves in tenanted accommodation, with a tapering support package and limited access to familial and professional networks. In addition, funding and resources available to care leavers and local authority responsibilities for care leavers have not always been clear. Despite the provisions in the Children Act 1989, many young people leaving care find themselves without the support they need to make effective transitions to adulthood.

On-the-spot questions

Reflect on your own experience of leaving home:

1 How old were you?
2 Did you really 'leave' or did you go back?
3 What support did your family give you?

Under the Children Act 1989 there were discretionary powers related to the welfare of care leavers which were rarely and inconsistently used and, in effect, care ended too abruptly for many young people or provision of support was disputed by the local authority. The barriers experienced by young people who leave care, accessing health, welfare, employment and educational opportunities, extend into their adulthood and for some care leavers the difficulties are exacerbated by their legal status and rights to reside in the UK. This chapter discusses recent legislation, regulations and guidance which can be drawn on by social workers to support, assist and empower care leavers.

The Children (Leaving Care) Act 2000

The explicit aim of the Children (Leaving Care) Act 2000 related to young people leaving care is to delay their transition from care to independence. The statutory scheme – incorporated in the Children Act 1989, the Children (Leaving Care) Act 2000, the Children and Young Persons Act 2008 – and the duties of the responsible local authority are designed to replicate 'the support that a good parent might be expected to give' (Wise et al., 2011:225).

Social work with young people leaving care straddles several issues including transition planning, education/employment and/or training needs, accommodation, finances and social/health well-being. Social workers in this area of practice need to have a firm grasp of the legislation and practice guidance available to them in order to ensure that they are fulfilling their obligations and that the young person accesses the support and resources they are legally entitled to. Studies of care leavers illustrate that the outcomes for this group of young people are poorer than for their peers on several measures: educational attainment; employment prospects; access to suitable housing/accommodation; health; and income (Johns, 2011). There are several aspects which should be addressed in order for care leavers to achieve the best possible outcomes. Wade and Johnson (2006) found several key factors for success for care leavers:

- settled care;
- thorough transition planning;
- assessment;
- review;
- delay in transition from care.

The legislation formalized the local authority duty to assign care leavers a personal advisor and prepare a pathway plan. Both of these measures are designed to ensure that planning for leaving care is instigated when the young person is approaching the age of 16 and that there is a named dedicated worker in place to assist the young person with the leaving care arrangements.

The leaving care scheme

The Children (Leaving Care) Act 2000 provides the framework for promoting better outcomes for care leavers across all services. The restricted life chances and poor outcomes for young people who leave care are well documented. The difficulties and barriers faced by care leavers were evidenced in an influential report: *Me, Survive, Out There?* (DH, 1999). This study drew attention to the complexity of the practical and legal issues faced by young people leaving care in the UK. Research findings more generally have stipulated the need for multi-agency interventions and the inclusion of housing and education departments in the preparation and planning for young people leaving care, emphasizing that care leavers are not solely the responsibility of the social services department. More recent research has highlighted the importance of addressing the health needs of care leavers, including mental health which can be adversely affected by transition from care to independence (Dixon, 2008). Support for care leavers was extended up until the age of 21 years and in cases where young people are in further or higher education until they are 25 years old.

The local authority

A key duty of local authorities in terms of their responsibilities towards young people in care is to prepare them for leaving care and provide support once they have left care (Brayne and Carr, 2010). As a starting point, in relation to care leavers it is important to remember that the local authority position is that of a parent. The concept of the *corporate parent* was introduced in the Children Act 1989 and in applying this to care leavers it falls upon the local authority to ensure that:

> care leavers are given the same level of care and support their
> peers would expect from a reasonable parent and that they are
> provided with the opportunities and chances needed to help
> them move successfully to adulthood (DfE, 2012).

In *R (SO) v London Borough of Barking and Dagenham* [2010] support for a young care leaver who was an asylum-seeker was disputed by the local authority. The judgment, however, argued that it is the clear intention of Parliament that local authorities provide and fund support for young people leaving care.

The responsible local authority is defined in s. 23A(4) Children Act 1989 and in the latest Care Leavers (England) Regulations 2010 as being the last authority which looked after an eligible or relevant child or young person. This responsibility extends to wherever a child or young person may be living in England or Wales and is designed to ensure continuity of care, thus sustaining familial and geographical links, and to prevent disputes between local authorities as to who is responsible for a care leaver who may move from one local authority area to another (Wise et al., 2011).

Eligible and former relevant children

The leaving care scheme introduced in the Children Leaving Care Act 2000 and the Children and Young Persons Act 2008 differentiated between the groups of young people leaving care and identified the range of responsibilities and duties local authorities have for these groups of children and young people. The Care Leavers (England) Regulations 2010 exclude children who return home permanently and those who received respite care (DfE, 2010). A former relevant child is entitled to provision until they reach the age of 21 years and these duties emphasise *contact, continuity* and *assistance.* Children who qualify for assistance also include those aged between 16 and 21 who are or were the subject of a special guardianship order.

An eligible child is defined in s. 1(19B)(1) Children Leaving Care Act 2000 as a young person in care aged 16 and 17 who has been looked after for (a total of) at least 13 weeks from the age of 14. Local authority duties include:

- appointing a personal advisor;
- preparing a written statement detailing how the needs of the child will be met;
- carrying out an assessment of need to determine what advice, assistance and support will be provided;
- preparing a pathway plan;
- reviewing the pathway plan regularly.

A relevant child (s. 2(23)(A) Children Leaving Care Act 2000) is a young person aged 16 or 17 who has already left care and who had been looked after for (a total of) at least 13 weeks from the age of 14, and had been looked after at some time while 16 or 17. The local authority duties include:

- appointing a personal advisor;
- preparing a written statement detailing how the needs of the child will be met;

- carrying out an assessment of need to determine what advice, assistance and support will be provided;
- preparing a pathway plan;
- reviewing the pathway plan regularly;
- safeguarding and promoting the welfare of the child (s. 23B(8) Children Act 1989);
- remaining in contact whether the child is in the area or not;
- continuing to provide a personal advisor and review the pathway plan;
- providing assistance, welfare, education or training, or accommodation.

A former relevant child (s. 2(23B) Children Leaving Care Act 2000) is a young person aged 18–21 who has been an eligible and/or relevant child in care or a young person who was looked after by a local authority either through a compulsory care order or remanded or accommodated by a voluntary agreement including under s. 20 Children Act 1989. The local authority duties include:

- remaining in contact whether the child is in the area or not;
- continuing to provide a personal advisor and review the pathway plan;
- providing assistance, welfare, education or training, or accommodation.

PRACTICE FOCUS

Tanya: care leaver entitlement

Tanya is 19 and she left foster care three years ago. She was in residential care for six years on a care order and is now living in a bedsit on which she pays rent and claims housing benefit for. Tanya would like to do a college course.

- Is Tanya an eligible, relevant or former relevant child?
- What support is Tanya entitled to under the leaving care scheme?
- What would you include in a pathway plan for Tanya?
- What housing options are available for Tanya?
- At what age will local authority support for Tanya cease?

The personal advisor

The local authority has a duty to appoint a personal advisor for an eligible child as soon as reasonably practicable. The personal advisor is the link between the eligible child and the local authority in matters related to their leaving care plans and assessments. All 'eligible', 'relevant' or 'former relevant' children will have a personal advisor who will make sure that they receive the care and support they need when they leave care. The Who Cares Trust explains what young people can expect from their personal advisor and emphasizes that young people should have a say in who is their personal advisor. The personal advisor may well be an employee of the local authority or an external agency, but what is clear is that they have a specific and independent role in relation to contributing towards the assessment which forms the pathway plan to preparing and supporting the young person leaving care.

> → **KEY CASE ANALYSIS** ←

R (G) v Nottingham City Council and Nottingham University Hospitals NHS Trust [2008]

G, a care leaver, was 18 years old. She had been in the care of the city council. G had a history of alcohol and drug abuse and self-harm, undoubtedly a very vulnerable young woman. In 2007 she became pregnant. The baby was due to be born in spring 2008 and was removed by social services at birth. The personal advisor role was compromised in this case and it was held that personal advisors need to have some independence. The city council was criticized for failing to comply with its statutory duties, the poor assessment which formed the basis of the pathway plan, and the plan itself which was deemed inadequate. In G's case her legal advisors argued that the pathway plan which the local authority had prepared was deficient and inadequate to the extent that it was unlawful.

The Children (Leaving Care) (England) Regulations 2001 set out the functions of personal advisors and their role: reg. 12 refers to functions of the personal advisor:

- to provide advice including practical advice and support;
- to participate in the assessment and preparation of the pathway plan;
- to participate in reviews of the pathway plan;
- to liaise with the responsible authority in the implementation of the pathway plan;
- to coordinate the provision of services and take reasonable steps to ensure the care leaver makes use of the services;
- to keep informed about the progress and well-being of the care leaver;
- to keep a written record of contacts with the care leaver.

The appointment of the personal advisor and their role in the pathway plan was also the subject of *R (on the Application of A) v London Borough of Lambeth* [2010]. The Care Leavers (England) Regulations 2010 stipulate that the personal advisor is an intermediary between the child and the local authority and is a participant in the production of the pathway plan, along with the young person, their social worker (if they have one) and other agencies (DfE, 2010). It was held that the plan drawn up by A's personal advisor was unlawful and the local authority was directed to produce a new plan in accordance with an expeditious timetable.

The personal advisor can be an employee of the local authority but cannot be the author of the pathway plan as this compromises their position in relation to their responsibilities towards the young person. This was the finding in *R (J) v Caerphilly County Borough Council* [2005].

In the cases referred to above, the local authorities were criticized for failing to ensure the independence of the personal advisor. In some cases, the personal advisor may need to challenge the local authority to provide services and support, and as such it is important that their role is separate and distinct from those of the social workers and other parties involved in the pathway-planning (see below) and support process for care leavers. The personal advisor can assist in several areas and their role includes ensuring that young people access services and support. As outlined in the introduction to this chapter, studies of care leavers have identified failings in the provision of housing, access to education, employment and training and welfare/benefits.

The pathway plan

The Children (Leaving Care) Act 2000 amended the Children Act 1989 to: 'improve the life chances of young people living in and leaving local authority care' (para. 1 Children (Leaving Care) Act 2000 guidance (DfE, 2010)). Every eligible child, former eligible child and former relevant child is entitled to leaving care provision. The social worker must carry out an assessment of the young person's needs in order to determine what advice, assistance and support the young person requires whilst they are being looked after and once they cease to be looked after. The personal advisor will also participate in preparing a pathway plan as soon as possible after the assessment. This is a detailed plan which should include an holistic assessment of the current and continuing needs of that young person. Regulation 8(2) of the Children (Leaving Care) (England) Regulations 2001 states that the pathway plan must set out how the responsible authority proposes to meet the needs of the child, the date by which this should be done and by whom, as well as outline any action to operationalize any aspect of the plan.

In *R (Birara) v London Borough of Hounslow* [2010], the young person sought a judicial review after the local authority's decision to cease support under the Children Act 1989 when the claimant turned 21. In this case, the young person had claimed and been refused asylum (she was later granted indefinite leave to remain) and the local authority had its own policy of not continuing support for care leavers after the age of 21. In this case, the pathway plan was deemed to be inadequate, lacking sufficient detail and included mistakes related to the claimant's immigration situation. In addition, the court found that the local authority could grant discretionary support past the age of 21 but had not considered acting outside of its policy to address the specific circumstances of the young person in question.

There are key elements of the pathway plan. The Children (Leaving Care) (England) Regulations 2001 require the following:

- the nature and level of contact and personal support provided to the young person and by whom;
- details of the accommodation the young person is to occupy;
- an education and/or training plan;
- details on how the local authority will assist the child or young person with employment or other purposeful activity or occupation;
- identification of support to enable the child or young person to maintain appropriate family and social relationships;
- a programme to develop independence/practical life skills;
- financial support to be provided to the child or young person, in particular where it is to be provided to meet his/her accommodation and maintenance needs;
- the health needs, including any mental health needs, of the child or young person and how they are to be met;
- contingency plans for action to be taken by the responsible authority should the pathway plan for any reason cease to be effective.

> → **KEY CASE ANALYSIS** ←

R (G) v Nottingham City Council and Nottingham University Hospital NHS Trust [2008]

In this case, the legal advisors argued that the pathway plan which the local authority had prepared for the care leaver was deficient and inadequate to the extent that it was unlawful. The city council was criticized for failing to comply with its statutory duties, the poor assessment which formed the basis of the pathway plan, and the plan itself which was deemed inadequate. Clearly, whilst there is a requirement that a young person preparing to leave care is involved in contributing to their pathway plan, the regulations are clear this should be in conjunction with their personal advisor, social worker and carers as well as family members where appropriate. In addition the pathway plan is a working document which requires ongoing review and development, and should be robust enough to withstand critical and, crucially, legal scrutiny. In this case the court noted that the local authority's duty during the assessment is not merely to identify the child's needs. It was stated that the 'assessment' should analyse and evaluate those needs so that a pathway plan could realistically set out in detail how the needs were to be met.

The pathway plan should be informed through ongoing consultation and discussion with the agencies and other individuals involved in providing care and/or support to the young person leaving care, including housing, education/training providers and health services, as well as the young person's family or kinship network where possible. Many of the young people involved in a study of care leavers by Wade (2008) were in contact with a family member when they left care, and not only did this relationship continue but, in many cases, it was perceived to be stronger in the follow-up period of the study by the young people themselves. Wade (2008) found that leaving care workers were not always effective at identifying kinship relationships in the lives of the young people they worked with or, indeed, in involving them in the pathway plan arrangements. This is despite the evidence which suggests that very often family members are willing and able to provide support to the young people. Even when the relationships between the young people and their families were difficult, it was still important to the young people that familial relationships continued and were supported. Clearly, creative and flexible family-based work can enhance the leaving care experiences and outcomes for young people.

Housing and homelessness

The Children (Leaving Care) Act 2000 amended the Children Act 1989 and imposed a duty on local authorities to provide support and accommodation for relevant children. This applies to those young people who are 16 and 17 years old. Where a young person over the age of 18 does not fulfil the definition of relevant child, the local authority only has a duty to assist them with accommodation and support. Those who are relevant or former relevant in full-time higher education or residential accommodation are also entitled to (or payment for) vacation accommodation.

The Children (Leaving Care) Act (2000) requires that 16/17-year-old relevant children are provided with or maintained in suitable accommodation and housing needs should be addressed before the young person leaves care and be included in the pathway plan. It is not deemed appropriate for 16/17-year-olds to have the responsibility of managing their own tenancy without support. Housing and social services should each play a full role in providing support and accommodation must be reasonably practicable for the young person given his/her needs. Crucially, bed and breakfast accommodation is not deemed to be appropriate except in an emergency (National Care Advisory Service, 2009). Where care leavers are in residential or higher/further education settings, the pathway plan should stipulate the arrangements for funding of vacation accommodation. Social services must provide accommodation during the vacations or pay the young person enough to secure accommodation for him/herself if the term-time accommodation is not available and this duty now remains until the care leaver's 24th birthday. Under the Housing Act 1996 and the Homelessness Act 2002 (Part VII Housing Act 1996), local authorities must secure suitable accommodation for a person who is eligible for assistance, is homeless (or threatened with homelessness within 28 days) or has a priority need for accommodation. The Homelessness (Priority Need for Accommodation) (England) Order 2002 extended the priority need categories to include homeless 18–20-year-olds who were in care at 16 or 17, except for those in residential or higher/further education settings requiring vacation accommodation, and homeless people over the age of 21 who are vulnerable as a result of being in care in the past.

Finances/welfare rights/budgets

Most 16/17-year-old care leavers will not be able to claim benefits. Therefore the young person will be reliant on their local authority for any income. Financial support provided will include the cost of accommodation, food and domestic bills, pocket money, transport for education and training, clothing and childcare. Essentially, the spirit of the leaving care scheme in this respect mirrors the way in which parents assist their children through the transition from home to independence. Weekly allowances are calculated by each local authority according to the young person's individual needs, but should not be less than the amount that the young person would receive if entitled to claim benefits. Lone parents or those unable to work because of illness or disability are still able to claim Income Support or Job Seeker's Allowance but not Housing Benefit; this applies whether they are still in care or have left care. The personal advisor should ensure that those who leave care at 18 and are entitled to claim benefits receive their full entitlement. If a care leaver moves to or from Scotland they will be able to claim benefits.

Employment/further and higher education

Educational attainment, financial support and assistance to continue in education are key developments in the provision of services to care leavers. Social services and other caring agencies need to liaise closely with schools, colleges and training providers. Connexions and other similar young people's services will help to fulfil the liaison role between school and social services. Local authorities now have a duty to assist former relevant children with the expenses associated with education and training. This duty runs until the young person has completed the programme of education and training agreed with the responsible local authority and set out in the pathway plan. Councils also have a duty to provide assistance to former relevant children with the expenses associated with employment. This provision covers contributions towards the cost of accommodation, which enables the young person to live near the place where he/she is employed or seeking employment.

This chapter has discussed the duties and responsibilities local authorities and social workers have to support young people through the complicated and lengthy process of leaving care. Leaving care is unlike leaving home and young people cannot always rely on the support from families and social networks which many people take for granted. The local authority as the *corporate parent* plays a key role in ensuring that local provision is accessible and appropriate. Delay in planning for care leavers can have significant negative impacts on young people who are already vulnerable and have experienced disadvantage and disruption in their childhood. The *pathway plan* is an important document which requires the involvement of agencies legally charged with supporting young people through their transition from care. The *personal advisor* plays a significant role in coordination and an advocacy role for young people leaving care. Child care social workers should ensure that they are liaising with leaving care workers/teams and personal advisors and should be able to recognize which children on their case loads are eligible for the different aspects of leaving care support.

Further reading

Charities and voluntary organizations – the Coram Children's Legal Centre and the Care Leavers Association produce fact sheets and booklets which outline the key duties of local authorities and what care leavers can expect from their personal advisor and how they can participate in the pathway planning process. A National Voice website is another useful resource which social workers and care leavers themselves will find useful – it gives clear information about the entitlements of care leavers. The Care Leavers Foundation and the Who Cares Trust promote the concerns of care leavers in the UK and are useful resources for personal advisors and young people themselves.

Dixon, J (2008) 'Young People Leaving Care: Health, Well-being and Outcomes' 13(2) *Child and Family Social Work* 207–17 draws attention to the neglect of the health needs of care leavers and makes a strong case for pathway-planning processes to include addressing the health issues of care leavers in an holistic way.

Wade, J (2008) 'The ties that bind: support from birth families and substitute families for young people leaving care' 38(1) *British Journal of Social Work* 39 stresses the importance of supporting and maintaining links between care leavers and their families and encouraging their involvement in the pathway planning process.

Wise, I et al. (2011) *Children in Need: Local Authority Support for Children and Families*. This is a key publication which includes references to case law and the change and developments in legislation related to care leavers in the UK. The chapter related to the leaving care scheme covers in detail the duties of local authorities towards young people leaving care, the role of the personal advisor and cases which have come before the courts where local authorities have failed in their duties towards care leavers.

7

CHILDREN WHO DISPLAY HARMFUL SEXUAL BEHAVIOUR

AT A GLANCE THIS CHAPTER COVERS:

- defining children with harmful sexual behaviour
- children's rights: Article 40 UNCRC
- the age of criminal responsibility
- assessment, community-based interventions and support for families
- specialist training for carers and professionals
- custodial sentences and treatment

Up to one-third of sexual abuse referred to statutory agencies is carried out by children and young people. Children who display harmful sexual behaviours and/or abuse other children are likely to be perceived as criminals on the one hand, and also as victims. Research suggests that this group of children needs effective, targeted support and/or treatment and many of them have been victims of some form of abuse themselves (Lovell, 2002) with females more likely to have been sexually abused than males (Hickey et al., 2008). Definitions of what is considered abusive are complex (Masson and Erooga, 2006) and the discussion in this chapter examines the legal perspectives relating to children and young people as laid out in the Sexual Offences Act 2003 and the support mechanisms which are contained within child care legislation and practice guidance.

What is harmful sexual behaviour?

Sexual exploration and experimentation are a normal part of child and adolescent development, and yet there are situations in which children and young people are sexually harmed by other children and young people. Sexually harmful behaviour is distinguished from normal sexual development if a sexual act is committed by a child or young person on another where there is no consent, and where threats or coercion are used. The widely accepted definition is: 'a minor who commits a sexual act with a person of any age, against the victim's will, without consent, in an aggressive, exploitative or threatening manner' (Ryan and Lane, 1997, cited in Hall, 2006:274). They are clearly children in need and are named as such in the DH (2000) *Framework for the Assessment of Children in Need and their Families*.

In assessing and distinguishing between experimental behaviour and behaviour that is abusive, consent, power, equality and authority are all key issues which those undertaking assessments need to take into

2009–2010	1912
2010–2011	1979
2011–2012	1888

Table 7.1: Sexual offences committed by children and young people

Source: Youth Justice Board Youth Justice Annual Statistics (2009/2010–2011/2012)

account. Issues regarding consent to sexual activity are laid out in the Sexual Offences Act 2003:

s. 4(1)

> A person commits an offence if
> (a) he intentionally causes another person (B) to engage in an activity,
> (b) the activity is sexual,
> (c) B does not consent to engaging in the activity, and
> (d) A does not reasonably believe that B consents.
>
> *Sexual Offences Act 2003*

Kane (2013) discussed several aspects of the behaviour which raised concerns and led to a YOT intervention. The behaviour was carried out on the pretext of befriending or babysitting younger children and included what would be described as grooming behaviour which was repeated, systematic and increased in intensity over time. It was also found that it was very difficult for children to admit that they had engaged in harmful sexual behaviour (personal correspondence).

On-the-spot question	Why might a child or young person continue to deny an allegation about them in respect of their harmful sexual behaviour?

The vast majority of those young people convicted of a sexual offence are males (98–99 per cent), however, there are children and young people who display harmful sexual behaviour under the age of 10 years and who are therefore below the age of criminal responsibility and much less is known about the gender and other demographics or characteristics of these children. Research on this issue has largely focused on clinical samples of children who have come into statutory provision and entered clinical treatment programmes. As these children are often in need, theirs and their family's engagement with services is voluntary. Several studies undertaken in the US and UK have found consistent patterns in the backgrounds of children and young people with harmful sexual behaviour which include chaotic and abusive backgrounds characterized by neglectful parenting owing to alcohol or substance misuse, a sexualized environment, and often sexual abuse experienced in childhood. There are some recent studies which have drawn on children and young people's perspectives and those of their parents/carers. HM Inspectorate of Probation (2013), in a recent report (discussed below), found that, although the behaviour can be extremely damaging to the children and young people who were the victims, the inspection also reported that children and young people with harmful sexual behaviour can and do respond to intervention and can be rehabilitated.

The UNCRC and children with harmful sexual behaviour

Article 40 UNCRC concerns the rights of children who are accused of committing crimes to be treated with dignity and have their age taken into account, as well as promoting their reintegration into society. Children have the right to be presumed innocent until proven guilty according to law, to be informed (as well as their parents/guardian/carers) of the charges which are being brought against them, and to have legal or other appropriate assistance in the preparation and presentation of their defence. This Article also includes the right to privacy, a fair hearing, appeal and the use of an interpreter if required. Meanwhile, states are required to provide a range of disposals and alternatives to institutional care, including: care, guidance and supervision orders; counselling; probation; foster care; education and vocational training programmes. The rights under Article 40 UNCRC are particularly relevant to children who have displayed harmful sexual behaviour as there is a public perception of those who sexually offend and a culture which sees the punishment for crimes being more acute when children are involved as victims. Moreover, the duty of the state to provide alternatives to custody is highly relevant here as there is clear evidence that custodial sentences for children and young people do not prevent them from re-offending.

Legislation and legal interventions

In England and Wales, we have more children and young people in the secure estate than many other European countries, despite the fact that imprisoning young people who are convicted of criminal offences does not reduce their offending behaviour or lessen their chances of returning to a Young Offenders Institution (YOI) (Pickford and Dugmore, 2012). There is a different approach in Scotland, guided by the principles of the Children (Scotland) Act 1995, which promotes a welfare response to children who commit crimes and diverts them away from the criminal justice system, courts and prosecution if they are under 12. The age of criminal responsibility in the rest of the UK is 10, an issue which the UN

Committee on the Rights of the Child commented upon in its monitoring report in 2008: 'It appears that England and Wales are falling far behind their European neighbours in consideration of the welfare of their young people.' (UNCRC, 2008)

On-the-spot questions	1 What are the implications for children who commit an offence at age 10?
	2 Are there greater implications for children who have displayed harmful sexual behaviour?

The law is interpreted strictly according to the Youth Justice Board (YJB) (2008) and children and young people over the age of 10 years who sexually abuse other children and young people are expected to take responsibility for their actions. A child who has displayed harmful sexual behaviour may have acted in some way sufficient to raise concerns. The definition of sexual abuse (HM Government, 2013) refers to a range of behaviours and specifically states that these may be acts committed by children.

Definition of sexual abuse

The definition of sexual abuse involves forcing or enticing a child or young person to take part in sexual activities, not necessarily involving a high level of violence, whether or not the child is aware of what is happening. The activities may involve physical contact, including assault by penetration (for example, rape or oral sex) or non-penetrative acts, such as masturbation, kissing, rubbing and touching outside of clothing. They may also include non-contact activities, such as involving children in looking at, or in the production of, sexual images, watching sexual activities, encouraging children to behave in sexually inappropriate ways, or grooming a child in preparation for abuse (including via the internet). Sexual abuse is not solely perpetrated by adult males. Women can also commit acts of sexual abuse, as can other children (HM Government, 2013).

The distinctions between children and young people engaged in consensual sexual activity and those who are demonstrating harmful sexual behaviour are discussed in relation to the way in which the Sexual Offences Act 2003 was developed (Waites, 2005). Child sex offences committed by children or young persons are defined in the Sexual Offences Act 2003 as follows:

s. 13

(1) A person under 18 commits an offence if he does anything which would be an offence under any of sections 9 to 12 if he were aged 18.
(2) A person guilty of an offence under this section is liable—
    (a) on summary conviction, to imprisonment for a term not exceeding 6 months or a fine not exceeding the statutory maximum or both;
    (b) on conviction on indictment, to imprisonment for a term not exceeding 5 years.

Sexual Offences Act 2003

Section 9 Sexual Offences Act 2003 deals with sexual activity with a child; s. 10 with causing or inciting a child to engage in sexual activity; s. 11 engaging in sexual activity in the presence of a child; and s. 12 causing a child to watch a sexual act. The penalties are different for offences committed by those under 16, and for those acts which are committed on children 13 years and under. The Sexual Offences Act 2003 contains several sections which differentiate between the various age groups – the protection of children under the age of 13 who are deemed not to be able to give sexual consent. The overriding concerns about the Sexual Offences Act 2003 with regard to children who have harmful sexual behaviour was that it should not unnecessarily criminalize them.

In England and Wales, the youth justice aspects of cases override the welfare aspects. The system in Scotland differs from England and Wales in key ways which prioritize the welfare of children who have demonstrated harmful sexual behaviour, recognizing that they are in need of support. Under the Children's Hearings (Scotland) Act 2011 there is a presumption that children are in need and that their welfare is paramount, along with an avoidance of prosecuting children under the age of 12. Yates (2013) argues that there are clear difficulties in terms of seeing children who have harmful sexual behaviour as criminals because, in many cases, children who have committed sexual offences have also experienced some kind of trauma and in Scotland the emphasis is on intervention based on welfare grounds (abuse or neglect). There may be issues for those over the age of 12 which are a mixture of welfare and safeguarding, including being in contact with the offender, a lack of parental care, significant harm, not attending school, and the child or young person may have committed other offences. There is thus a reluctance to proceed with prosecution as the child may then have a sexual offence on record.

In a case in Scotland described by Yates, the child had committed a sexual offence against another child but the panel was reluctant to proceed on the basis of the offence. Instead, it proceeded with an intervention which was based on issues related to parental care. However, the parents disputed that this was required and then the child withdrew the statement and denied that the offence had taken place, which effectively meant that there was no case to answer. There was a view that the child needed to work with the agency around his harmful sexual behaviour and yet, because of the principles of proceeding on welfare grounds, there was no opportunity to work with him. In the event of the child being charged with an offence, there would still be no intervention with him and he would continue to pose a risk (Yates 2013, personal correspondence). In addition to the issue of no intervention, the system also defines a child as a sex offender at age 12 with little acknowledgment that this behaviour can be addressed and changed through effective and specialist intervention.

The disposals available in England and Wales will depend on the severity of the offence and whether or not there is a decision to prosecute the child or young person, and a consideration of the best interests and the welfare of the child or young person would inform this decision (Pickford and Dugmore, 2012). There are several other factors which need to be taken into account in relation to sentencing. As outlined above, in relation to the system in Scotland it can be difficult to intervene and work with a child or young person who denies their behaviour and the UNCRC provides for the right to be innocent until proven guilty. Thus, an assessment of need based on welfare issues might enable a more effective and timely intervention. The length of time of the assessment and subsequent intervention also needs to be taken into account – an adequate amount of time to assess and work with the issues is essential in this respect and a referral order (maximum 12 months) may be the most appropriate sentence. However, there are clear tensions in this respect as any conviction will remain on the child or young person's record and affect their future employment or training prospects.

Assessment and support for children and parents

Because they are defined as children in need, those children who come to the attention of professionals as a result of their harmful sexual behaviour are entitled to an assessment under s.17 Children Act 1989 (see Chapter 1). It may not be possible for the young person to live with their family during the assessment process as they may pose a risk to other children in the household. The assessment model used should be a holistic one which recognizes the importance of family networks to the child. The assessment model will also need to consider issues in regard to how much supervision is needed for future planning and support. *Working Together to Safeguard Children* (DfE, 2013c), which replaces *the Framework for the Assessment of Children in Need and their Families* (DH, 2000) (see Chapter 1), is also drawn on by local authorities and outlines the roles and responsibilities of the various agencies, including the requirement to have local procedures in place to deal with cases. In practice, the most suitable option is for co-working between children's social services and YOT workers, however, this is not always possible. Hackett et al. (2013) state that between a quarter and a third of all sexual abuse coming to the attention of the child welfare and criminal justice systems in the UK and North America is carried out by children and young people. There is also a division between children who demonstrate harmful sexual behaviour being viewed as a threat and a risk and being known therefore to criminal justice agencies such as YOTs and, conversely, being known to social workers, but not always to both. The concerns about how best to intervene and support children with harmful sexual behaviours are the same for both social workers and YOT workers, and include the need for specialist support and training. The widely cited and influential NCH Action for Children study (NCH, 1992) advised that cases involving children with harmful sexual behaviour should ideally be co-worked so as to reduce the risk of collusion, challenge denial or minimization tactics, reduce the inevitable stress and potential for isolation in working on such cases, and provide opportunities for learning and development of expertise and skills in this complex area. HM Inspectorate of Probation (2013) made several recommendations for LSCBs related to the identification of children likely to display harmful sexual behaviour (i.e. those who have been sexually abused), providing early intervention and support, undertaking joint assessment, and promoting liaison and communication with multi-agency public protection arrangements (MAPPA). In any event, a holistic assessment is required which focuses on the needs of the child or young person and does not solely focus on the harmful sexual behaviour.

In many cases, although not all, the local YOT will be involved in the assessment and provision of services to children who have displayed harmful sexual behaviour. YOTs are multi-agency teams responsible for the supervising of children and young people who are subject to pre-court interventions and statutory court disposals (HM Government, 2013). There is good evidence that community-based specialist support and intervention for children who have displayed harmful sexual behaviours is effective and can address the behaviour (HM Inspectorate of Probation, 2013) and the advice to YOTs is to recommend that additional interventions to address the harmful sexual behaviour are commissioned in the event that young people are sentenced to custody, as there is a limited range of specialist provision in the secure estate to support and work with young people who have been convicted of sexual offences (YJB, 2013).

AIM2 assessment framework

> **PRACTICE FOCUS**
>
> The framework adopts a partnership approach, which is essential for the development of effective practice. It incorporates the concepts of the DH *Framework for the Assessment of Children in Need and their Families* (2000) used by children's services, social care and other agencies, as well as the 'Asset' framework used by YOTs. Its use is intended to fit within the timescales agreed by the criminal justice and child welfare systems. The AIM2 initial assessment model designed by Print et al. (2007) is the first stage in gathering and analysing information, which will assist practitioners to consider what further assessments and interventions might be required to support the young person and their parents/carers. The framework provides a model to assist all professionals within children's services social care, YOTs and other agencies or services which have contact with children to conduct an initial assessment in order to:
>
> - identify potential risk of re-offending;
> - in child protection terms, identify risk to either the young person or their actual/potential victim(s);
> - identify the young person's needs;
> - assess the young person's motivation and capacity to engage in services and plans;
> - identify the capacity of the parents/carers to support the young person;
> - suggest priorities for initial response;
> - consider referral to the MAPPA;
> - identify levels of supervision required.

The AIM2 assessment framework and procedures are designed to assist professionals in assessing children who are alleged to have committed a sexual assault or admitted to undertaking sexually harmful behaviour.

Social work practice issues

Hackett and Masson (2006) adopted a service-user perspective in their research with young people who have displayed harmful sexual behaviour. They acknowledge the difficulty in this approach and the scarcity of service-user empowerment approaches in research around sexual aggression generally, given the emphasis on controlling and managing those who sexually offend so as to reduce risk and punish offending behaviour.

HM Inspectorate of Probation (2013) reports on an inspection of the effectiveness of the multi-agency response to children and young people who had received a sentence for a sexual offence and were being supervised in the community in England and Wales. It examined the quality of the work undertaken with these children and young people and its outcomes explored how the different agencies had worked together. The study included interviews with children, young people and their parents and found that many of them had already been known to children's social care services but their sexualized behaviour had either been missed or not been deemed significant enough to warrant an intervention. This was described in the report as a 'lost opportunity'. The report also found that there was a long delay between the offence being disclosed or admitted and the sentencing of the child or young person – an average of eight months. This had consequences for the intervention which would be needed to start to address the child or young person's harmful sexual behaviour. Little or no work could be carried out if the offence was denied. The report also found reluctance amongst social services and YOTs to share information with education providers and limited examples of holistic multi-agency assessment. As a result, in many cases the underlying reasons for the harmful sexual behaviour were not analysed. There were gaps in communication and information-sharing between agencies, although communication and information-sharing tended to be most effective when formal systems were in place, i.e. child protection meetings. On a more positive note, the children and young people and their parents felt they had been kept informed and advised of progress with assessment and intervention by the workers and had felt involved in the processes. The inspection also found good examples of family support work, but again little evidence of action to address the complexity that characterized the family circumstances of some of the children and young people which was linked to the harmful sexual behaviour (HM Inspectorate of Probabtion, 2013).

Hawkes (2009) points out that the avoidance of naming the behaviour as harmful and using euphemisms (e.g. an unpleasant incident, inappropriate sexual behaviour) serves only to reduce the likelihood of an effective and accurate risk assessment. Avoidance of naming the behaviour occurs sometimes so that a placement is not compromised, however, this makes the work of carers much more difficult and potentially puts any other children in their care at risk. It is also collusive and conveys a message to the child about shame and secrecy which reinforces their guilty feelings and reluctance to engage with an intervention. If a child is being placed in foster care, social workers must be very clear about the behaviour and advise the carers. If the foster carers have their own or look after other children, then social workers need to be able to make a decision about managing the risk that these children may be vulnerable (Hawkes, 2009; Masson et al., 2013). It is clear that children and young people who have displayed harmful sexual behaviour will not want to be identified as such for fear of community reprisals and so the pride and belonging that many service-user groups feel is not experienced by young people who have harmful sexual behaviour, on the contrary, they feel shame and distress (Hackett and Masson, 2006).

Hackett and Masson argue that, whilst a sensitive task and one fraught with tension and emotive issues, eliciting the perspectives of young people with harmful sexual behaviour can help to contribute to effective professional interventions in the future. Hackett and Masson's (2006) study identified that trustworthiness and reliability were prerequisites for a positive experience of intervention, particularly from specialist workers who were deemed to be truthful and provided space to open up about difficult issues and feelings. In contrast, professional interventions were criticized when professionals misled or gave inaccurate advice, or left the young people feeling abandoned by not visiting (social worker) or not following up on actions after an interview (police). Continuity of worker was an important aspect for parents and young people as were clear explanations, including 'abuse clarification', to parents about the harmful sexual behaviour, and about the process once the professionals were involved. In addition, parents indicated that the length of time the intervention would go on for should be clarified and in some cases reduced as they felt that it had gone on for too long and had a detrimental impact on their child. Responses from parents in this study also suggest that social workers and other professionals lacked understanding of the emotional burden and difficulty for parents in coming to terms with the sexual abuse their child had carried out. Responses from young people in the study highlight the importance of help-seeking and accessing support to stop the behaviour. In situations where children have harmful sexual behaviour and are in need of support, this support needs to be extended to parents who can reinforce positive interventions and therapeutic work, as well as take measures to protect their children and reduce risk factors.

RESPOND

RESPOND is a service which works with young people with sexually harmful behaviour. Young people with learning disabilities account for between 30–50 per cent of all young people with harmful sexual behaviours. Many of their clients who display sexually harmful behaviours have experienced sexual or physical abuse, neglect, domestic violence or dysfunctional and emotionally distant parenting. Interventions to address such experiences are often not identified quickly to prevent dysfunctional pathways into harmful behaviours. The clinical interventions for victims of sexual assault by children and young people may also differ. However, it is crucial that the clinical and therapeutic interventions for children and young people displaying the harmful sexual behaviour are not delayed as early intervention has shown to be effective in reducing the risk of repeat behaviours (Hawkes, 2009).

Specialist services, assessment and interventions

Specialist training for carers is advocated by Masson et al. (2013) who report on research undertaken with carers who looked after young males who had demonstrated harmful sexual behaviour and, in some instances, had been convicted of offences in this regard. Specialist training is also advocated for YOT workers and social workers in this area. Kane (2013) discussed her experiences of working in a YOT with children and young people who had been convicted of a sexual offence or had displayed harmful sexual behaviour and advises caution in terms of preparing for sessions and debriefing afterwards. Co-working and joint assessment and intervention were also recommended as this would ensure that practitioners could offer support to each other and challenge, too, where there was a risk of collusion. In addition, it was felt to be important for workers to have an awareness of their impact and the impact on them of the nature of the offence, whilst also addressing the behaviour sensitively but robustly and allowing the child or young person to move on (Kane, 2013, personal correspondence).

GMap is an independent organization which provides services for young people who display inappropriate sexual behaviours. GMap works with their families, carers and their professional networks. They offer training to professionals and have been involved in developing and implementing assessment tools and approaches to working with children and young people with harmful sexual behaviour. Training for workers undertaking assessment and intervention in this area of work is essential and particularly where evidence suggests that a significant number of children and young people who display sexually harmful behaviour or have been convicted of a sexual offence have learning difficulties. Training would be required on the assessment of learning needs to inform therapeutic practice, including: intervention planning and treatment delivery; adapting models and tools for individual and group-work; identifying and addressing barriers in assessment and treatment and setting realistic treatment targets; developing strengths-based practice which empowers young people with learning needs to make positive choices, whilst also promoting healthy sexual development and functioning; and engaging with the support networks of young people to capitalize and extend their learning and skills development (GMap, 2013).

Custodial sentences

A limited range of specialist provision is available for young people convicted of sexual offences within the secure estate. The decision as to where to place a young person will depend on several issues. Often young people will present with a high level of 'at risk factors' and consideration should be given to where they are most appropriately placed and any young person convicted of a sexual offence will be assessed using a specialist assessment tool. The YJB will always support a community-based intervention programme for young people, should their risk be properly managed in a community setting, and strongly advises YOTs not to solely recommend custody in order that a young person will receive specialist intervention as this cannot be guaranteed and this practice potentially could result in their offending-related needs not being met. In secure children's homes and secure training centres, the provision available differs between establishments. For young people who are 15–17 years old, and where it is deemed appropriate for them to be placed into a YOI, the YJB has contracted with the Lucy Faithfull Foundation (LFF) to provide a service for young people with sexual convictions in four of the male YOIs. The LFF is a child protection charity operating across the UK, specializing in safeguarding children from sexual abuse.

The LFF will only work with young people who have been sentenced to an order for sexual offences. The service provided by LFF includes a range of comprehensive assessments and interventions designed to meet the young person's individual offending-related needs delivered according to their circumstances. Where possible, this involves close work with families and liaison with YOT workers to assist with future planning and resettlement (YJB, 2013).

> **KEY CASE ANALYSIS**

R v Williams (Christopher) [2012]

In 2010, Williams aged 17 was convicted of charges under s. 13 Sexual Offences Act which related to 13 child sex offences (committed by children or young persons). He was sentenced to 14 months' detention in a YOI. A sexual offences prevention order was also made for a period of 10 years and his name was included in the relevant list maintained by the Independent Safeguarding Authority under the Safeguarding Vulnerable Groups Act 2006.

The charges all involved online sexual offences against children he had made contact with on his computer over the internet (via chat rooms) – young girls from various parts of the world – between 17 November 2007, when he was 15, and 25 January 2010, when he was 17. He had contacted 100 girls over the internet, some of whom had made statements to the police. He enticed the young girls to take their clothes off and pose for him. Williams stored the images and films, but there was no evidence of sharing or distribution to others or to suggest that anyone else had access to his computer.

In a pre-sentence report, Williams was assessed by the probation service as being at high risk of committing serious offences in relation to children. However, it was indicated that he would benefit from extensive intervention which would be required to reduce the risk presented in the community. This intervention, said the author of the presentence report, could be undertaken via a determinate custodial sentence or a community order with 24 months' supervision to include a one-to-one sexual offending programme.

The appeal case was that the judge failed to apply the appropriate sentencing guidelines. In particular, he applied the guidelines that applied to those over 18 rather than those which imposed a more lenient sentencing regime for young people under 18, which are to be found in Part 7 of the guidelines (Sentencing Guidelines Council, 2003). The appeal argued that a custodial sentence should have both been shorter and suspended and, indeed, combined with a supervision order that would provide for a suitable programme for the appellant to undertake. The starting point for any form of sexual activity, non-penetrative or penetrative, not involving any aggravating features, is a community order.

In this case, the appeal was allowed because it was agreed that the original judge had not applied sentencing guidelines correctly. It also acknowledged that there was a maximum of two years' age difference between the age of the offender and the child victims. The different sentencing requirements for those who are 17 or under mean that community-based treatment programmes can be implemented, especially given that these programmes are not always available in the secure estate.

This chapter has provided an overview of the key issues related to the assessment of children with sexually harmful behaviour. The intervention and responses by social workers and other agencies is governed by the Children Act 1989 and also by the statues related to criminal justice. As discussed, children in England and Wales as young as 10 years of age may be convicted of a sexual offence and so a degree of caution and sensitivity is required when undertaking work in this area as the implications of a conviction for a sexual offence as a child will still be felt when the child becomes an adult. The process of assessment is thus crucial, as is adherence to the UNCRC regarding the treatment of young people accused of criminal offences. The provision of services to children and their families has been found wanting and so it is important that social workers and those working in YOTs familiarize themselves with the assessment approaches and interventions available to them in order to ensure that children receive the most appropriate and timely support and interventions to address their behaviour before it becomes entrenched.

Further reading

Hackett, S and H Masson (2006) 'Young people who have sexually abused: what do they (and their parents) want from professionals?' 20(3) *Children and Society* 183–95. This well-focused research study examines the support issues and the tensions for families in coming to terms with understanding and responding to the harmful sexual behaviour of their child.

Pickford, J and P Dugmore (2012) *Youth Justice and Social Work* examines the youth justice system and engages in debates related to the criminalization of children and young people and outlines the role of the YOT.

Waites, M (2005) *The Age of Consent: Young People, Sexuality and Citizenship*. This book traces the history of debates and legislation related to young people's sexual consent and, in particular, the changes implemented in the Sexual Offences Act 2003.

8
CONCLUSION

This concluding chapter draws together some of the common themes and issues and makes a plea for social workers in child care and initial assessment teams and those working with children and young people in community and statutory services to assess and recognize that the needs of children and young people change over time, are not constant and often cannot be determined by chronological age. This chapter acknowledges that children and young people are often fully aware of how their needs can be met and children's rights perspectives which provide for this approach to assessment and provision of support are often the most effective.

In Chapter 1, the legal framework for the provisions in the Children Act 1989 and the provisions in the Children Act 2004 were introduced. Section 17 Children Act 1989 together with the *Framework for the Assessment of Children in Need and their Families* (DH, 2000) are the key ways in which social work assessment practice is formed in the UK. The difficulties in assessment of children in need relate to the subsequent allocation of resources and the lack of intervention. As noted, whilst there has been an emphasis in UK government policy since 1989 towards early intervention, the provision of community-based interventions is determined by local authority resources which are under increasing pressure. The powers and duties which determine the roles and responsibilities of local authorities in respect of children in need and their families cannot be avoided. This chapter also identified some of the practical steps and approaches which are used in assessment practice and are informed by s.17 Children Act 1989 and subsequent legislation.

Chapter 2 discussed which children we mean when we talk of children in need of support in the UK. This chapter also provided an overview of who works with children in need of support and in what context. The key examples of community-based services – a Sure Start project and an FGC service – illustrate that accessibility and location are crucial in providing services for children and their families. It was also clear, as discussed in this chapter, that children and their families appreciated and benefited from having access to one service which could signpost or assist them in accessing more specialist support. It thus falls to social workers in this area of work to ensure that they are familiar with local provision, access routes and referral pathways for children in need and their families. Many children in need of support will not require statutory intervention under s. 17 Children Act 1989, however, community and family support mechanisms require resourcing and the local authority duty in this respect is discussed here.

The importance of the UNCRC in shaping UK legislation was discussed in Chapter 3. The duty on local authorities to ensure that children's rights are upheld has not always been prioritized in practice and the UN Committee on the Rights of the Child raised concerns about several groups of children who were treated less favourably in the UK. There are clear tensions in relation to ensuring that children in need are included in the processes of decision-making about their welfare and have their rights promoted when being assessed for or receiving support. Their participation (Article 12 UNCRC) and their rights to family life (Article 8 UNCRC) being two areas where the interests of children are often superseded. The difficulties in aligning practice with children's rights perspectives were discussed in this chapter as well as potential solutions.

Chapter 4 examined social work assessment practice with separated children and UASCs. As discussed, since the start of the twenty-first century there has been a tightening of border controls which has made it increasingly difficult for children to come to the UK in the first place. Once they arrive here, separated or unaccompanied children are entitled to the same provisions as any other child in the UK, regardless of their status and entitlement to be in the UK. In addition to undergoing assessment and inquiries from the UKBA in relation to age and status, separated and unaccompanied children must also navigate their way through a complex welfare system to access health, education and housing support. As discussed, a key element of the assessment of need for separated or unaccompanied children is in relation to their need for stability and security given the nature of their arrival. Settlement needs are often neglected until leave to remain is confirmed, however, as Wright (2012) has identified, a triple-planning approach can often resolve the potential for uncertainty in terms of settlement at least in the short term. Appeal court rulings in this area have successfully challenged local authorities which negate or avoid their responsibilities toward separated and unaccompanied children. In addition, there are now established protocols and guidance for age assessment which provide a greater degree of security for children where there is doubt about age.

Chapter 5 discussed the legal issues which inform and shape the assessment of needs for children with disabilities and their families. As discussed, because of the changing nature of disability and its impact on children and their families, children with disabilities require ongoing assessment and regular review. Education, health, housing, and access to leisure provision require ongoing review to meet these changing needs and to ensure that, wherever possible and in the child's best interests, they can remain in the care of their family. The provisions set out in legislation for carers can greatly assist parents who are caring for their children under considerable pressure. The transitions between child and adult services are potentially difficult processes and ensuring that children's best interests are promoted is key here, too, particularly as their wishes and aspirations may depart from what parents want for their child. Advocacy for children with disabilities to ensure that their views are promoted in discussions about transition planning is crucial and should be included as part of the pathway planning process.

The complexity of assessing need and promoting the interests of young people who are care leavers was discussed in Chapter 6. In the first instance, it is vital that transition planning begins at an early stage and that the various parties are clear about their roles and responsibilities and the duties of local authorities in relation to the different categories of care leavers. The principles of the legislation clearly accept that leaving care is a process and not a one-off event. In effect, care leavers should receive the level of support that any child growing up and leaving home would expect from their families. As such, legislation has been implemented and provides resources for care leavers including housing, education, health and other welfare benefits. Appeal courts have ruled in favour of care leavers and have been hugely critical of local authorities who evade their duties in this respect. The disadvantaged starting point for young people leaving care is well established in research and social workers and personal advisors play a central role in leading assessment practice for care leavers and accessing resources for them in the community.

Chapter 7 discussed the needs of children who have displayed harmful sexual behaviour. The potential for this group of children in need to have unmet needs is high, as reported in HM Inspectorate of Probation (2013), and, coupled with the risk that such children are viewed as criminals, suggests that assessment of need and implementation of therapeutic and other forms of treatment is crucial. Given that the research in the UK and in the US suggests that children who display sexually harmful behaviour have often been the victims of abuse and/or neglect themselves, their need for sensitive and specialist support and intervention is clear. The support needs are provided by trained and highly experienced carers and therapists who draw on a wide set of skills and approaches aimed at managing any risks these children present and addressing the harmful behaviour and preventing any repeat offending.

Summary

It is clear that the legal framework, guided by international conventions and domestic law and guidance, provides for the many different eventualities which may be experienced by children who are in need of support. The groups discussed in this book are by no means the only children in need of support. Children in need include those who provide care for their parents who are mentally ill or disabled, or have substance misuse or alcohol dependency problems. Children who have witnessed or experienced domestic violence and children with emotional and behavioural problems may all at one time or another meet the legal criteria for children in need services. What appears to be crucial is that an assessment of need is followed up by an intervention. It is clearly not sufficient or in children's best interests to assess that there is no risk of harm and then close the case. Being *in need* is a legal status and the Children Act 1989 and subsequent legislation has maintained this position whilst also recognizing that early intervention can prevent issues from escalating further. The issues discussed in this book clearly illustrate that being in need is not a one-off event. Whilst it is not acceptable for children and families to be part of a revolving-door system or be subjected to multiple assessments, it is important for social workers to recognize that some children will move in and out of the category of need and others will require more intensive and resource-heavy intervention at different points in time.

For children with disabilities and particularly those with deteriorating conditions or significant health problems, the impact on families caring for children cannot be underestimated and social workers play a key role in terms of liaison and consultation with the multiple agencies involved in the lives of these children. For children who have come to the UK to seek asylum, the circumstances of their arrival may be an indication of their need for support, advice and assistance to settle and claim refugee status and less about their vulnerability to being trafficked. The status and legal entitlements of these children are often neglected and the courts have been clearly in favour of promoting their rights and entitlements despite legal challenges by local authorities. Care leavers often start their journey to independence at an earlier age than their peers who live with their families. The route to independence is fraught with personal, emotional and economic challenges which are frequently exacerbated for care leavers who often do not have close supportive familial ties to rely on. The social work role here is key to ensuring that entitlements to assistance, training, education and health are available and accessible for these young people as they navigate their way into adulthood. Perhaps most controversially, children who display harmful sexual behaviour are also a group of children who are in need and their rights to have support and assistance are clear in the legal framework and in the UNCRC. A children in need intervention for these children is especially important where a criminal justice approach to punishment might eclipse their need for detailed thorough assessment and the provision of therapeutic support to prevent reoccurrence of their behaviour.

There are several key points which can be drawn from the discussion in this book and about the groups of children who fall into the category of need:

- Early intervention can provide assistance when it is needed and can prevent issues from escalating and having a greater and more detrimental impact on children and their families.
- Children in need and their families will sometimes need ongoing support and the intensity of support may shift as needs and circumstances change.
- In all respects and in relation to all groups of children in need, thorough and holistic, theoretically informed assessment is central to ensuring that needs are identified and services put in place to address these and support children and their families.
- Knowledge of and adherence to the legislation and statutory guidance will only serve to improve social work practice with children in need of support.
- Where there is any doubt about the legal position in relation to a child in need, then social workers have a responsibility to seek advice from official legal sources.
- Recognizing the evolving capacities of children and actively seeking their participation and involvement in decisions about their care and welfare is a duty and, as such, a central feature of social work undertaken with children in need.

USEFUL WEBSITES

A National Voice
www.anationalvoice.org/about/about-anv

Care Leavers' Association
www.careleavers.com

Child Poverty Action Group
www.cpag.org.uk

Children and Young People Now
www.cypnow.co.uk

Contact a Family
www.cafamily.org.uk

CORAM Children's legal Centre
www.childrenslegalcentre.com

G-Map
www.g-map.org

Immigration Law Practitioners Association
www.ilpa.org.uk

National Youth Advocacy Service
www.nyas.net

Refugee Council
www.refugeecouncil.org.uk

The Council for Disabled Children
www.councilfordisabledchildren.org.uk

UNCRC
www.unicef.org/crc

GLOSSARY

Advocacy
Children and young people's access to advocacy is established in legislation (Children Act 1989, Children (Leaving Care) Act 2000 and Adoption and Children Act 2002). Advocacy provides a support mechanism, a voice for looked after children, unaccompanied children and care leavers, amongst others, to make representations about the quality of the care and support provided by their responsible authority.

Age dispute
The age of children and young people who arrive in the UK is disputed when they cannot provide documentation which establishes their age or the documentation is not considered genuine by the UKBA. These children and young people may not appear to be the age they are claiming based on physical appearance and are likely to be age-assessed to determine their immigration status and decide who has responsibility for providing accommodation and support.

Age assessment
Age assessment refers to the procedures used by authorities who establish the chronological age of an individual. Age assessment procedures must be in line with the UNCRC, and be *Merton* compliant, taking into account the best interests of the child and, where there is doubt or uncertainty, treat him or her as a child.

Care leaver
A care leaver is a young person who has been 'looked after; for a defined period of time by a local authority'. There are three categories of care leavers which determine their entitlement to ongoing support and advice: eligible child, relevant child and former relevant child.

Child in need
'For the purposes of this Part a child shall be taken to be in need if: (a) he is unlikely to achieve or maintain, or to have the opportunity of achieving or

maintaining, a reasonable standard of health or development without the provision for him of services by a local authority under this Part; (b) his health or development is likely to be significantly impaired, or further impaired, without the provision for him of such services; or (c) he is disabled, and "family", in relation to such a child, includes any person who has parental responsibility for the child and any other person with whom he has been living.' (s. 17(10) Children Act 1989)

Children in need

'It shall be the general duty of every local authority ... (a) to safeguard and promote the welfare of children within their area who are in need; and (b) so far as is consistent with that duty, to promote the upbringing of such children by their families.' (s. 17(1) Children Act 1989)

Children in Need: Annual Census

'... an annual collection of data on children who have been referred to local authority social care services because their health or development is at risk of being significantly impaired without additional support' (www.gov.uk/ children-in-need-census).

Detention

Separated and unaccompanied children and sometimes those in families are held in secure accommodation whilst their status is established. The detention of children should be avoided and used only as a last resort and for the shortest possible period of time. There have been cases where children have been detained as adults when their age has been incorrectly assessed.

No order principle

This principle was designed to prevent cases coming to the courts if it was better not to make an order: 'Where a court is considering whether or not to make one or more orders under this Act with respect to a child, it shall not make the order or any of the orders unless it considers that doing so would be better for the child than making no order at all.' (s.1(5) Children Act 1989)

Pathway plan

The pathway plan assesses the needs of a young person who is leaving care and records the actions and services required to respond to these needs. The pathway plan documents the provision of support during the young person's transition to adulthood and independence. The pathway plan should be reviewed every six months until the young person turns 21 years of age, or beyond if they remain in education.

Personal advisor
A personal advisor is appointed by the local authority for an 'eligible', 'relevant' or 'former relevant child'. The personal advisor will make sure that the care leaver receives care and support and ensure that reviews of the pathway plan take place and that it is kept up to date.

Threshold criteria
A legal concept which, once established, informs a family court that on a balance of probabilities a child is at risk of or is likely to suffer significant harm which is attributable to one of the following: a) the care given to the child, or likely to be given if the order were not made, not being what it would be reasonable to expect a parent to give; or b) the child being beyond parental control (s. 31(2)(b) Children Act 1989). If there is insufficient evidence that the child meets the threshold criteria then a s. 17 Children Act 1989 child in need assessment will ensue. The court will only consider a care or supervision order if the threshold criteria are met. Whether a child is likely or not to suffer harm will also form part of the criteria for the initiation of a s. 47 Children Act 1989 investigation. Thresholds of harm for a s. 47 investigation are defined by the LSCB.

Transition planning
Children in need, those who are disabled, unaccompanied children and those who are care leavers require support during their transition from childhood to adulthood especially where they will continue to be in receipt of social services. Effective transition planning includes several agencies, lead/key workers and crucially the involvement of children, young people and wherever possible their families

UN Convention on the Rights of the Child
An international human rights treaty, the UNCRC grants all children and young people a comprehensive set of rights. The UNCRC came into force in the UK on 15 January 1992. The UNCRC applies to children who are defined as being from birth to 18 years old and sets out what every child needs to have a safe, happy and fulfilled childhood regardless of their sex, religion, social origin, and where and to whom they were born.

Wishes and feelings
Section 17(4) Children Act 1989 requires 'the local authority to: (a) ascertain the child's wishes and feelings regarding the provision of those services; and (b) give due consideration (having regard to his age and understanding) to such wishes and feelings of the child as they have been able to ascertain'.

BIBLIOGRAPHY

Ball, C (2014) *Looked After Children* (Basingstoke: Palgrave Macmillan)

BBC (2013) 'Angry clashes take place during food banks debate' www.bbc.co.uk/democracylive/house-of-commons-25431723

Bianchini, K (2011) 'Unaccompanied asylum-seeker children: flawed processes and protection gaps in the UK' 37 *Forced Migration Review* 52–3 www.fmreview.org/sites/fmr/files/FMRdownloads/en/non-state.pdf

Braye, S and M Preston-Shoot (2012) *Curriculum Guide: Social Work Law* (London: The College of Social Work/Higher Education Academy) www.tcsw.org.uk/uploadedFiles/TheCollege/Media_centre/CG_Law.pdf

Brayne, H and H Carr (2010) *Law for Social Workers* 11th edn (Oxford: Oxford University Press) ch. 9

Broach, S, L Clements and J Read (2010) *Disabled Children: A Legal Handbook* (London: Legal Action Group/Council for Disabled Children)

Broadhurst, K, D Wastell, S White, C Hall, S Peckover, K Thompson, A Pithouse and D Davey (2009) 'Performing "Initial Assessment": Identifying the Latent Conditions for Error at the Front-Door of Local Authority Children's Services' 40(2) *British Journal of Social Work* 352–70 www.publicservices.ac.uk/wp-content/uploads/broadhurst-et-al_2009-performing-initital-assessment_.pdf

Butler-Sloss, E (1988) *Report of the Inquiry into Child Abuse in Cleveland 1987* Cm 412 (London: Department of Health and Social Security/HMSO)

Children England (2010) *The Role of Third Sector Innovation: Personalisation of Education and Learning – Children England submission to the Office of the Third Sector* (London: Children England) www.childrenengland.org.uk/upload/Children%20England%20submission%20OTS%20personalisation%20in%20education%20and%20learning.pdf

Cleaver, H and S Walker with P Meadows (2004) *Assessing Children's Needs and Circumstances: The Impact of the Assessment Framework* (London: Jessica Kingsley)

Continyou (2013) *Pyramid Club* www.continyou.org.uk/what_we_do/pyramid/about

Coram Children's Legal Centre (2012) *Seeking Support: A Guide to the Rights and Entitlements of Separated Children* (London: Coram)

CPAG (2013) *Child Poverty Facts and Figures* (London: CPAG) www.cpag.org.uk/child-poverty-facts-and-figures

Crawley, H (2010) *Chance or Choice: Understanding Why Asylum Seekers Come to the UK* (London, Refugee Council)

Crawley, H (2012) *Child First, Migrant Second: Ensuring that Every Child Matters* (London: ILPA)

Crawley, H, S Bolton, N Finch, A Harvey, B Sandhu, S Shutter, M Tabib, L Woodall and C Yeo (2012) *Working with Children and Young People Subject to Immigration Control: Guidelines for Best Practice* 2nd edn (London: ILPA) www.ilpa.org.uk/data/resources/14627/12.04.25-ilpa_child_gdlines_2nd_ed.pdf

CRIN (2013) 'The Convention' www.crin.org/en/home/rights/convention

Dalrymple, J and J Hough (eds) (1995) *Having a Voice: An Exploration of Children's Rights and Advocacy* (New York: Venture Press)

Davies, M (ed.) (2012) *Social Work with Children and Families* (Basingstoke: Palgrave Macmillan)

DfES (2004) 'Get it Sorted: Guidance – Providing Effective Advocacy Services for Children and Young People Making a Complaint under the Children Act 1989' (Nottingham: DfES) http://webarchive.nationalarchives.gov.uk/20130401151715/http://www.education.gov.uk/publications/standard/publicationdetail/page1/gis%2004

DfE (2010) *Planning Transitions to Adulthood for Care Leavers: Statutory Guidance of the Care Leavers (England) Regulations* vol. 3 (London: DfE)

DfE (2012) *The CAF Process* (London: DfE) www.education.gov.uk/childrenandyoungpeople/strategy/integratedworking/caf/a0068957/the-caf-process

DfE (2013a) *Characteristics of Children in Need in England: Year Ending March 2012* (London: DfE) https://www.gov.uk/government/publications/characteristics-of-children-in-need-in-england-year-ending-march-2012

DfE (2013b) *Information on the Numbers of Children Referred and Assessed by Children's Social Services for the Year Ending March 2012* (London: DfE) www.gov.uk/government/uploads/system/uploads/attachment_data/file/167406/sfr27-2012v4.pdf.pdf

DfE (2013c) *Working Together to Safeguard Children: A Guide to Inter-agency Working to Safeguard and Promote the Welfare of Children* (London: DfE) www.gov.uk/government/publications/working-together-to-safeguard-children

DfES (2001) *Special Educational Needs: Code of Practice* (London: DfES) http://webarchive.nationalarchives.gov.uk/20130401151715/https://www.

education.gov.uk/publications/standard/publicationdetail/page1/dfes%
200581%202001

DfES (2010) Working Together to Safeguard Children: A Guide to Inter-
agency Working to Safeguard and Promote the Welfare of Children
(London: DfES) http://webarchive.nationalarchives.gov.uk/20130401151
715/https://www.education.gov.uk/publications/eorderingdownload/
00305–2010dom-en–v3.pdf

DH (1999) *Me, Survive, Out There?* (London: DH)

DH (2000) *Framework for the Assessment of Children in Need and their Families*
(London: The Stationery Office)

DH (2003) (Local Government Circular (2003)13) 'Guidance on accommo-
dating children in need and their families' (London: DH)

Dixon, J (2008) 'Young people leaving care: health, well-being and
outcomes' 13(2) *Child and Family Social Work* 207–17

EHRC (2013) *UN CRC Report on UK Performance* (Cardiff/Glasgow/London:
EHRC) www.equalityhumanrights.com/human-rights/our-human-rights-
work/international-framework/un-convention-on-the-rights-of-the-
child/un-crc-report-on-uk-performance

Family Rights Group (2013) 'Family group conferencing' (London: Family
Rights Group) www.frg.org.uk/involving-families/family-group-conferences

Fell, P and D Hayes (2007) *What Are They Doing Here? A Critical Guide to
Asylum and Immigration* (Birmingham: Venture Press)

G-Map (2013) www.g-map.org

Hall, S (2006) 'Children with harmful sexual behaviours – what promotes
good practice? A study of one social services department' 15(4) *Child
Abuse Review* 273–84

Hackett, S and H Masson (2006) 'Young people who have sexually abused:
what do they (and their parents) want from professionals?' 20(3) *Children
and Society* 183–95

Hackett, S, H Masson, M Balfe and J Phillips (2013) 'Community reactions to
young people who have sexually abused and their families: a shotgun
blast, not a rifle shot' *Children and Society* (early view online article)
DOI:10.1111/chso.12030

Hawkes, C (2009) *Sexually Harmful Behaviour in Young Children and the Link to
Maltreatment in Early Childhood: Conclusions from a UK Study of Boys
Referred to the National Clinical Assessment and Treatment Service (NCATS),
a Specialist Service for Sexually Harmful Behaviour* (London: NSPCC) www.

nspcc.org.uk/Inform/research/findings/sexually_harmful_behaviour_in_young_children_wdf70757.pdf

Hendrick, H (1994) *Child Welfare England 1872–1989* (London: Routledge)

Hickey, N, E McCrory, E Farmer and E Vizard (2008) 'Comparing the developmental and behavioural characteristics of female and male juveniles who present with sexually abusive behaviour' 14(2) *Journal of Sexual Aggression* 241–52

HM Government (2007) *Statutory Guidance on Making Arrangements to Safeguard and Promote the Welfare of Children under Section 11 of the Children Act 2004* http://webarchive.nationalarchives.gov.uk/201304011 51715/https://www.education.gov.uk/publications/eOrderingDownload/DFES-0036-2007.pdf

HM Government (2013) *Working Together to Safeguard Children* online version www.workingtogetheronline.co.uk/chapters/chapter_one.html#assessments

HM Inspectorate of Probation (2013) *Criminal Justice Joint Inspection Examining Multi-Agency Reponses to Children and Young People Who Sexually Offend: A Joint Inspection of the Effectiveness of Multi-agency Work with Children and Young People in England and Wales Who Have Committed Sexual Offences and Were Supervised in the Community* (London/Manchester: HM Inspectorate of Probation) www.justice.gov.uk/downloads/publications/inspectorate-reports/hmiprobation/joint-thematic/children-yp-who-sexually-offend-report.pdf

Holland, S (2011) *Child and Family Assessment in Social Work Practice* 2nd edn (London: Sage Publications)

Holt, K (2014) *Child Protection* (Basingstoke: Palgrave Macmillan)

Horwath, J (2011) 'See the practitioner, see the child: *The Framework for the Assessment of Children in Need and their Families* ten years on' 41 *British Journal of Social Work* 1070–87

House of Commons Education Committee (2012) *Children First: The Child Protection System in England* Fourth Report of Session 2012–13 vol. 1 www.publications.parliament.uk/pa/cm201213/cmselect/cmeduc/137/137.pdf

House of Commons Library (2013) 'Ending child immigration detention' Standard Note: SN/HA/5591 (London: House of Commons) last updated: 2 January (author M Gower, Home Affairs Section)

Jenkins, P (1995) 'Advocacy and the UN Convention on the Rights of The Child' in J Hough and J Dalrymple, *Having a Voice: An Exploration of Children's Rights and Advocacy* (New York: Venture Press)

Johns, R (2011) *Using the Law in Social Work* 5th edn (Exeter: Learning Matters)

Johns, R (2014) *Capacity and Autonomy* (Basingstoke: Palgrave Macmillan)

Jordan, L (2012) 'The legal foundations of family support work' in M Davies (ed.), *Social Work with Children and Families* (Basingstoke: Palgrave Macmillan)

Joseph Rowntree Foundation (2008) *Housing and Disabled Children* (York: Joseph Rowntree Foundation) www.jrf.org.uk/publications/housing-and-disabled-children

Kane, H (2013) Personal correspondence, 31 May 2013 (Helen Kane is Enhanced Family Court Advisor CAFCASS in Lancashire)

Kohli, R (2007) *Social Work with Unaccompanied Asylum Seeking Children* (Basingstoke: Palgrave Macmillan)

Kvittingen, A V (2010) *Negotiating Childhood: Age Assessment in the UK Asylum System* Working Paper Series No 67 (Oxford: Refugee Studies Centre) www.rsc.ox.ac.uk/publications/working-papers-folder_contents/RSCworkingpaper67.pdf

Laming, Lord (2003) *The Victoria Climbié Inquiry* (London: House of Commons Health Committee/HMSO)

Larkins, C, N Thomas, D Judd, J Lloyd, B Carter, N Farrelly, R Hendry and L Davis (2012) *'We Want to Help People See Things Our Way': A Rights-based Analysis of Disabled Children's Experience Living with Low Income* (London/Preston: Children's Commissioner for England/University of Central Lancashire) www.childrenscommissioner.gov.uk/content/publications/content_731

Lovell, E (2002) *Children and Young People Who Display Sexually Harmful Behaviour* (London: NSPCC) www.nspcc.org.uk/inform/research/briefings/sexuallyharmfulbehaviour_wda48213.html

Masson, H, S Hackett, J Phillips and M Balfe (2013) 'Looking back on the long term fostering and adoption of children with harmful sexual behaviours: carers' reflections on their experiences' *British Journal of Social Work* 1–18

Masson, J and M Erooga (2006) *Children and Young People Who Sexually Abuse Others: Current Development and Practice Responses* 2nd edn (London: Routledge)

Matthews, A (2012) *Landing in Dover: The Immigration Process Undergone by Unaccompanied Children arriving in Kent* (London: Office of the Children's Commissioner) www.childrenscommissioner.gov.uk/content/publications/content_556

Montgomery, H and M Kellett (eds) (2009) *Children and Young People's Worlds: Developing Frameworks for Integrated Practice* (Bristol: Policy Press)

Munro, E (2011) *The Munro Review of Child Protection: Final Report. A Child-Centred System* www.gov.uk/government/publications/munro-review-of-child-protection-final-report-a-child-centred-system

Munro, E (2012) *Progress report: Moving Towards a Child Centred System* (London: DfE) www.gov.uk/government/publications/progress-report-moving-towards-a-child-centred-system

Nando, S and V Hughes (2012) *No Way Out, No Way In: Irregular Migrant Children and Families in the UK,* (Oxford: COMPAS Research Report, University of Oxford) www.compas.ox.ac.uk/fileadmin/files/Publications/Research_projects/Welfare/Undocumented_children/No_Way_Out_No_Way_In_May_2012.pdf

National Care Advisory Service (2009) *Journeys to Home: Care Leavers' Successful Transition to Independent Accommodation* (London: National Care Advisory Service)

NCH (1992) *The Report of the Committee of Enquiry into Children and Young People who Sexually Abuse Other Children* (London: NCH)

Newbigging, K and N Thomas (2010) *Good Practice in Social Care with Refugees and Asylum Seekers* (London: Social Care Institute for Excellence) www.scie.org.uk/publications/guides/guide37/files/guide37.pdf

OFSTED (2011) *Inspection Report for Sure Start Talbot and Brunswick Children's Centre* (Manchester: OFSTED) www.ofsted.gov.uk/inspection-reports/find-inspection-report/provider/ELS/23107

Pickford, J and P Dugmore (2012) *Youth Justice and Social Work* 2nd edn (Exeter: Learning Matters)

Print, B, H Griffin, A R Beech, J Quayle, H Bradshaw, J Henniker and T Morrison (2007) *AIM2: An Initial Assessment Model for Young People Who Display Sexually Harmful Behaviour* (Manchester: AIM Project)

Read, J, L Clements and D Ruebain (2006) *Disabled Children and the Law: Research and Good Practice* 2nd edn (London: Jessica Kingsley)

Refugee Council (2005) *Ringing the Changes: The Impact of Guidance on the Use of Sections 17 and 20 of the Children Act 1989 to Support Unaccompanied Asylum Seeking Children* (London: Refugee Council) www.refugeecouncil.org.uk/assets/0001/5583/RingingthechangesJanuary2005.pdf

Refugee Council (2012a) *Not A Minor Offence: Unaccompanied Children Locked Up as Part of the Asylum System* (London: Refugee Council) www.refugeecouncil.org.uk/assets/0002/5945/Not_a_minor_offence_2012.pdf

Refugee Council (2012b) *Refugee Council Briefing on Home Office Asylum Statistics for 2012* (London: Refugee Council) www.refugeecouncil.org.uk/assets/0001/5778/Asylum_Statistics__Aug_2012.pdf

Sentencing Guidelines: Council (2003) *Sexual Offences Act: Definitive Guidance* http://sentencingcouncil.judiciary.gov.uk/docs/web_SexualOffencesAct_2003.pdf

Shelter (2013) *Nowhere to Go: The Scandal of Homeless Children in B&Bs* (London: Shelter) http://england.shelter.org.uk/__data/assets/pdf_file/0009/727290/Nowhere_to_go_CHRISTMAS_2013.pdf

Stein, M (2006) 'Research review: young people leaving care' 11(3) *Child and Family Social Work* 273–79

Thomas, N (2002) *Children, Family and the State* (Bristol: Policy Press)

Trussel Trust (2013) 'UK Foodbanks' www.trusselltrust.org/foodbank-projects

Turney, D, D Platt, J Selwyn and E Farmer (2011) *Social Work Assessment of Children in Need: What Do We Know? Messages from Research* (London: DfE) www.gov.uk/government/publications/social-work-assessment-of-children-in-need-what-do-we-know-messages-from-research

UN Committee on the Rights of the Child (2008) UNCRC www2.ohchr.org/english/bodies/crc/docs/AdvanceVersions/CRC.C.OPAC.GBR.CO.1.pdf

UNHCR (2008) *Guidelines on Determining the Best Interests of the Child* (Geneva: UNHCR) www.unhcr.org/4566b16b2.html

Wade, J (2008) 'The ties that bind: support from birth families and substitute families for young people leaving care' 38(1) *British Journal of Social Work* 39

Wade, J and J Dixon (2006) 'Making a home, finding a job: investigating early housing and employment outcomes for young people leaving care' 11(3) *Child and Family Social Work* 199–208

Waites, M (2005) *The Age of Consent: Young People, Sexuality and Citizenship* (Basingstoke: Palgrave Macmillan)

Welbourne, P (2012) *Social Work with Children and Families. Developing Advanced Practice* (Routledge. London)

Westwood, J L (2012) 'Constructing risk and avoiding need: findings from interviews with social workers and police officers involved in safeguarding work with migrant children' 21(5) *Child Abuse Review* 349–61

Who Cares Trust (2014) www.thewhocarestrust.org.uk/pages/whats-a-personal-advisor.html

Wise, I et al. (2011) *Children in Need: Local Authority Support for Children and Families* (London: Legal Action Group)

Wright, F (2012) 'Social work practice with unaccompanied asylum-seeking young people facing removal' *British Journal of Social Work* 1–18 DOI:10.1093/bjsw/bcs175

Yates, P (2013) Personal correspondence, 23 May 2013 (Peter Yates is a Doctoral Student in the School of Social and Political Science at Edinburgh University)

YJB (2008) *Young People who Sexually Abuse* http://yjbpublications.justice.gov.uk/en-gb/Resources/Downloads/KEEP_YPSA.pdf

YJB (2013) 'Young people convicted of sexual offences' (London: YJB) www.justice.gov.uk/youth-justice/custody/specialist-resources/young-people-convicted-of-sexual-offences

INDEX